Soft-Tip Darts for the New Player

A Quiver of 3

TIMOTHY R. BUCCI

1663 LIBERTY DRIVE, SUITE 200
BLOOMINGTON, INDIANA 47403
(800) 839-8640
WWW.AUTHORHOUSE.COM

© 2005 Timothy R. Bucci. All Rights Reserved.

No part of this book may be reproduced, stored in a retrieval system, or transmitted by any means without the written permission of the author.

First published by AuthorHouse 10/12/05

ISBN: 1-4208-7920-0 (sc)
ISBN: 1-4208-9337-8 (e)

Library of Congress Control Number: 2005907792

Printed in the United States of America
Bloomington, Indiana

This book is printed on acid-free paper.

Disclaimer

The purpose of this manual is to educate and entertain. The author and the publisher endure neither liability nor responsibility with respect to any loss or damage caused or alleged to be caused directly or indirectly by the information contained in this book.

Every effort has been made to make this book as complete and accurate as possible. However, there may be mistakes, both typographical and in content. Therefore, this text should be used only as a general guide and not as the ultimate source of information with regards to the subject of soft-tip darts.

Dart skill is not developed overnight. Anyone who elects to undertake and pursue this sport must expect to invest much time and effort without any guarantee of success.

It is also not the purpose of this manual to reprint all the information that is otherwise available to dart enthusiasts, but to complement, amplify, and supplement those other sources. For further information regarding the sport of darts, please check your local library.

Table of Contents

Dedication	ix
Forward	xiii
Darts for the Masses	1
How to Choose A Set of Darts	5
Practice, Practice, Practice!	15
Developing Your Darts Math Skills	31
Good Mechanics for Success	39
The Power of Imagery	47
The Art of Confidence	53
A Tale From Inside "The Zone"	57
How to Build a Great Darts Team	63
Clothes That Can Break Your Game	69
Know Thy Opponent	73
Winning Strategies	89
This and That	99
Throwing Darts in Springfield, Illinois	105
In Thanks	113
The Official Player's Guidebook of the National Dart Association	117

Dedication

"You can do better than me. You could throw a dart out the window and hit someone better than me. I'm no good!"
~ **George Costanza**

Man, I was the worst beginner I've ever seen play the game of darts. No kidding. It felt good just to hit the board, let alone a target on it. Imagine comedian Chevy Chase fumbling with a steel-tip dart and dropping it into his foot. Only then will you begin to understand how terrible I was. Thank God for soft-tip!

And I wasn't *just* a horrific player. That wouldn't quite underscore the true essence of my early abilities at the line. To be as precise as possible, one must take the gloves off and just say it: I was a serious menace to the success of my team. But I'm getting slightly ahead of myself....

This story really started in 1991 with the start of a new job. There, I got to know a guy named Greg Johnson. Admittedly, when it comes to meeting new people I am not the most personable, but I distinctly recall being amazed at the quick development of our friendship. Greg is one of those disarming personalities who, I'm certain, could have made Stalin laugh. He truly has a gift for breaking down barriers.

Not long after we started working together, my darts addiction took root when his 301 team needed a substitute player. Not knowing I was about to eat a treble hook – from which I have yet to escape – I agreed to help out.

I was very fortunate in that Greg was a tireless and patient teacher. Good-natured, skilled, confident, and knowledgeable about the game, he never got upset with me or any other shooters, and – most importantly – he was always a gracious sportsman, win or lose.

I learned a lot and have him to thank for nurturing my interest in this sport. Since he introduced me to those first matches years ago I have always tried to model my game, behavior, and positive attitude after his (still failing too often, I fear).

As I watched Greg in those early, formative seasons, well beyond those first nights when hitting a target was my only concern, something started to sink into my wee brain. I began to realize anyone could throw a dart. Some would even be more accurate then others. But, it's the way we behave and treat those around us in the heat of the match that marks the difference between a great player and a low-browed fool with a good arm.

Another friend, Craig Crawford, has a term for players like Greg. He calls them "Darts Ambassadors." Whether they're world champions or not, these are the real leaders in this game. They show by example how we should all shoot and behave in the world of dart's social, yet competitive circles. These are the people who best represent this game and the players in it to the "outside world."

For darts to grow and thrive in America, I believe it is better if the players in this sport are known as good people, as opposed to being just good marksmen. Too often we are perceived to be drinkers and fighters – dark and dingy tavern dwellers – who throw darts only to laze our time away between the drinking and fighting. These descriptions, of course, are gross untruths.

Not often enough are we recognized as passionate competitors, organized sportsmen, or charitable with regard to any number of causes, both local and national. All Darts Ambassadors – because they're good people first, and darters second – carry a positive image every day to a world that hardly knows us, or knows us incorrectly. Frankly, it's high time this image is changed.

According to the St. Louis Post-Dispatch, in a single year some 20 million people play at least one game of darts in the United States. As opposed to league and tournament players, a large percentage of this group would be categorized as the casual or recreational player. These are the people on the cusp of involvement in our future leagues and tournaments. If we are to change our image and help to foster the growth of our chosen sport, we must begin with them. A handshake, some encouragement, and a simple "good game" may be all that's required for them to join us more often.

I recognize I was fortunate to have someone support, influence, and guide me in so many positive ways when I first started. Therefore, for that first invitation to be a substitute on his team, for being the first Darts Ambassador I ever knew, for teaching me this sport, and for all the positives and good sportsmanship lessons I learned from him along the way, this book is dedicated to my old, sage friend, Greg Johnson. He helped me develop more then just my skills in this game ... he helped improve the man inside the player, too. Thank you, Greg.

Forward

"The discipline of the writer is to learn to be still and listen to what his subject has to tell him."
~ **Rachel Louise Carson**

QUIVER (kwiv'-er), *n.*: A case or sheath for carrying arrows; a part of the warrior, foot soldier, charioteer, and huntsman's ordinary equipment.

Regarding the odd title, "A Quiver of 3," I have always drawn parallels between modern day darters and the bowmen of old – both the archers and their crossbow brethren. In fact, for years I used a crossbow warrior in the masthead of a mock darts, newsletter called, "The Marksman." While it was only a single "cover" page, inevitably its focus was on a recent darts match between my archrival (and friend … shhhhhhh!) Rick Hesse and me. To say I took a great deal of literary license in the retelling of these matches is an understatement of the highest order.

Add to this, films about that legendary Sherwood-ian, Robin Hood, always held my attention as a boy, especially during the scenes where he'd precisely split arrows already embedded in a target. As an adult, perhaps that fixation on accuracy might explain some of the lure of darts for me. At any rate, the title, "A Quiver of 3," pays homage to these films, my twisted journalistic past, and my immense passion for the sport of darts.

This publication is intended to help new players develop the skills to more quickly become better shooters, ask them to think about some issues in unexpected ways, build upon proven strategies, and hone their sportsmanship.

In darts there is no university degree, no hallowed hall to learn the intricacies involved with winning, and no master under whose tutelage we might study for years to develop our game. To learn, we must simply immerse ourselves in practice, both league and tournament play and, if we're lucky, we'll also be blessed with some insight from those who have discovered a few things before us.

I will be the first to admit it: I have harvested some excellent bits of wisdom from some truly amazing players. As a student of this game I find myself constantly looking for ways to improve, making it a habit to look for something new from every outing. Many a time I could be seen in my car before heading home from a match or tournament, jotting down ideas, details of events, and questions I felt were important to the focus of this book.

"How does she hold her dart?"

"What are the benefits of that stance?"

"He closed a number without being ahead on points. Why?"

To the new player: Make it a point to observe like this, too, and don't hesitate to ask questions of *anyone*. Trust that the pro-level players in your community will be more then happy (oftentimes flattered) to answer your questions and discuss your observations. Remember, part of what helped them rise to the top of the heap is that *they* observed and asked questions of better players who came before them, too.

No matter where the information I've collected here originated, I'm sure you and your fellow darters will find enough ideas to generate many discussions among you. Thank you for your interest. I hope you enjoy the book.

Game on!

Darts for the Masses

"During my eighty-seven years I have witnessed a whole succession of technological revolutions, but none of them has done away with the need for character in the individual or the ability to think."
~ **Bernard Mannes Baruch**

The soft-tip darts revolution began in 1975 with a small machine shop owner named Rudy Allison. While traveling through Ireland, Allison stayed in the coastal town of Wicklow. There, spending several hours with the locals playing steel-tip darts, Allison noticed that – while enjoying the game immensely – the task of manual "chalking (where points are totaled on a small chalkboard nearby)" seemed to interrupt the flow of the game.

"Why hasn't someone developed a method to score darts automatically?" he wondered. After all, electronic scoring could already be found in pinball machines and elsewhere. Why couldn't someone transfer that technology (somehow) to the sport of darts?

The idea began to consume him. When Allison came back to the United States, he'd already developed a rough idea for a dartboard that would automatically calculate scores.

Over a year's period, and with a small number of employees under his direction, the dartboard began to take shape. For the first, exploratory boards, thousands of holes were drilled through their fascia by hand, with an electrically connected "bed of nails" beneath this perforated surface. Next, using plastic dart tips that were covered in a foil-like substance, the thrown dart would hit a target on the board and the dart would close the circuit. A rudimentary calculator then applied the target's point value to an overall score.

They even went so far as to develop a mechanical arm that would sweep across the fascia and drop the darts onto a conveyor belt to return them to the player, much like what happens in the sport of bowling. But this was quickly abandoned. After all, unlike bowling, players only had to walk eight feet to retrieve their arrows.

Based on this new product, and with a little financial backing from a company called National Latex, Allison created Arachnid, Inc. (so named after a spider's web, which resembles a dart board). Development on the soft-tip board crept along, and in 1977, Mike Tillery and Paul Beall bought the company.

Ultimately, because of some design limitations, targets on the board had to be enlarged to some extent. But there was a long-term, unexpected benefit to this, as it's believed these changes helped contribute to the sport's popularity explosion in the mid-to-late 1980s. The modifications made games faster overall, less tedious for the beginner and thereby encouraged players to play – and pay – more often.

But, prior to that upsurge, sales of the soft-tip dartboard remained sluggish, due to an industry of hesitant amusement operators. They simply weren't convinced of its success. After all, steel-tip darts had quite a loyal following, and getting players interested in these new boards appeared to be a daunting task.

That notion changed dramatically, though, as there was a fortunate convergence for Arachnid in the early 1980s. Two enthusiastic sales representatives were added to the Arachnid team, Sam Zammuto and Marcio Bonilla, and shortly after their arrival electronic dartboard sales shot upward. Zammuto was an avid darter who learned to play in England during his stint with the U.S. Air Force. Ultimately, he became a world-caliber darts player, while Bonilla was already a well known figure in the amusement trade and a former Foosball world champion (inducted to the Table Soccer Hall of Fame in 1986).

With their help, a thriving Arachnid strengthened its grip on the sport, holding a variety of seminars and consultations to help distributors and operators develop leagues and tournaments all over the country to promote their boards. Soft-tip darts was taking off.

Management changes came in 1989 when John Martin, a successful Rockford, Illinois businessman, acquired Beall's share of the company. But by then – noticing Arachnid's burgeoning success in this niche market – other amusement companies were tossing their own electronic dartboards into the fray, like the Scorpion dartboard by Merit Industries and the Cougar dartboard by Valley, Inc (later known as Shelti, Inc.).

Today, soft-tip darts has become an integral part of the amusement industry, generating millions of dollars across the country. According to "Play Meter" magazine's 2004 state-of-the-industry report, the average, weekly take for an electronic dartboard was $36, which translated to a total of $131 million in revenue for the year ... just on darts!

And the rest, as they say, is history.

How to Choose
A Set of Darts

"Aim at the sun. You may not reach it, but your arrow will fly higher than if aimed at an object on level with yourself."
~ **Joel Hawes**

When my wife Annie first began playing darts in 1993, I got her a set of 16g tungsten Rangers. I have always liked Rangers, but this set seemed perfect for her – not just for their tungstenian slimness – but because the character of the barrels would foster a grip she could replicate easily each time she held a dart.

Annie is truly a natural, hand-eye coordinated player. For someone so new to the sport, she was on the path to becoming very good, very quickly, averaging at least one Bull's Eye every round in our count-up games. She nailed her first hat trick within two weeks of playing. I was amazed. I can still remember how excited she was.

But, alas, being the fashion conscious individual that she is, Annie decided she wanted "prettier darts" and bought a set of gold, nondescript, torpedo-shaped Predators (these are out of production now, I believe). No knurling, little character, just smooth and tapered. But, boy, were they ever pretty. We held a small ceremony each time she opened the case.

Long story short, her game went straight down the toilet. The problem was she couldn't hold these darts the same way twice. Thankfully, once she saw the light and dumped them, her game resurfaced, too.

Is there a moral to the story? Yes. Think less of pretty, and put more emphasis on what's functional. Darts are tools, after all, not ornaments.

Now, let's break down a dart and discuss its various sections.

The Barrel

After the time when wood was used to make darts, there was an era when brass was the metal of choice for barrels in the dart world. Its benefits were that it was a strong, resilient, and malleable metal. Manufacturers relied on it almost exclusively. Even today, steel-tip players who played in the "brass era" have a certain fondness for the feel of it.

Although pricey, tungsten darts began to strike a chord in the 1960s. According to John Lowe (to name a few of his titles: World Champion – 1979, 1987, 1993; World Master's Champion – 1976, 1980; World Matchplay Champion – 1984), the era of tungsten was ushered in around 1970 by world champion, Barry Twomlow (News of the World Champion – 1969; North American Open Mixed Double's Champion, with Anne Specht – 1976; Unicorn Darts America Open Double's Champion, with Paul Lim – 1985) and his sponsor, Unicorn, the world-renowned darts manufacturer. The impetus: Twomlow realized that too often his fat, brass darts already embedded in the small T20 (triple 20) were regularly deflecting his later darts intended for that same target. He reasoned that reducing the volume of his darts (more specifically, the width and length of the barrels) would improve his scores. In discussing the observation with Unicorn, the manufacturer embraced the idea and developed a slimmer tungsten dart set for him.

Since tungsten is three times the density of brass, the length of Twomlow's new barrels were reduced, their width dropped by half and, ultimately – based on his further successes at the line – the world stage began to push out brass and adopt this new metal as the de facto standard. From this one idea, tournament players and attendees noted a near instant leap in the occurrences of the "ton-80" feat (three triple-20s, equaling 180 points). Twomlow and Unicorn, it seems, had changed the world of darts forever.

Tungsten was inexpensive, too. Unfortunately, it had one big drawback. While it's very dense, it's also very brittle. Therefore, nickel is commonly added to create an alloy that can better tolerate the abuses tungsten products are bound to undergo – darts included. Lowe raves about the advent of the titanium/tungsten barrel in the late 1980's, as he claims it better mimics the "old school" brass darts in its feel, yet retains all the advantages of tungsten.

Personally, I have adopted a brass/tungsten model (the darts on this book's cover are similar to what I shoot with today) because, as stated earlier, brass is very malleable and lends itself to giving me a slight "wave" shape to my barrel. The barrel is still thin enough for me to enjoy tight groupings, too.

Whether it's titanium, nickel, brass, or any other metal for the new darts player, the differences between these metals when combined with tungsten do not matter. Simply grab a set with some good barrel character and start getting the game under your belt.

Tungsten darts will typically vary between 80% and 90% purity, dependent on the manufacturer and the model. However, be careful with darts containing the higher tungsten content, as these can still break under the right conditions, like bounce-outs onto a hard floor. If your set has been out in the cold for a long period of time (like in your car overnight during winter months), warm them up adequately to avoid breaking the barrels if they should hit the floor, ruining your set.

In terms of dart weight, soft-tip darts generally weigh 14 grams (g), 16g, or 18g each, although good, lighter models are still available out there. As manufacturers continue to make the dartboard's fascia and its underlying components sturdier, these weights are certain to graduate upward to levels more commonly used by steel-tip throwers.

Weight wise, while heavier darts might improve your control, they require a little more effort to get them to your intended target in the same way you threw lighter models. Weight is just another comfort consideration for every player. If you've found a dart that feels good in your grip, and your reseller has 14g, 16g, and 18g versions of it available, you're in luck! The ability to test each of these sets to find the optimum balance between the issues of effort, control, and release should prove very fruitful.

From my own experience (and this is merely a personal preference), heavier darts are easier for me to control then lighter ones. But, check the weight restriction of your local amusement company, too, and make sure you know the weight rules for any tournaments you are considering.

If the tournament or league has set a weight limit at 18g and an opponent believes your darts are hitting the board too loudly, indicating their heaviness (or they happen to see your open darts case is marked with a sticker that reads "20g"), be prepared: your darts could get weighed.

At best, you may be required to forfeit all wins in the match up to that point, and use a partner's lighter darts for the remainder (considering how familiar we get with our little arrows, this could be a major blow to your game). At worst, ready yourself to get ejected for violating tournament or league rules. Amusement companies are not amused (pun intended) with people who damage their expensive dartboards with darts that are too heavy. Considering the asking price for a new, top of the line model is over $3,100 these days, one can hardly blame them.

"But what are the characteristics of a good barrel?" you may ask. Now *that's* a good question!

The true measure of a barrel is how good it feels in *your* hand, provided the barrel is not too long (more about length later).

There should be enough features on the barrel for you to know how you should hold and throw it with consistency.

Remember the story about my wife, Annie, at the beginning of this chapter? A good barrel will provide enough definition so you can return to – and replicate – your grip without dwelling on this every time you grasp a dart. **At the line, you should be concentrating on your targets, <u>NOT YOUR TOOLS</u>.**

The process of preparing to throw your darts should be effortless. Without looking, how does the dart feel as you grasp it? Is it comfortable in your grip? Standing at the line, preparing to throw the dart, do your thumb and index fingers consistently return to the same spots on the barrel with every throw?

And what about the release? Are you required to adjust your natural throw too much to correct a dart's wobbly flight, or does it fly straight like an arrow would? Do you notice a lot of "bounce outs?" If you do, there is too much waffle in the dart's approach.

If you like the weight and characteristics of a barrel, usually everything else can be replaced. Don't just let the pretty colors on the case or the set's breakable/replaceable components influence your purchasing decision. If you do, there's a good chance you'll be back again to buy what works, as opposed to what looks good. There's nothing wrong with taking pride in the way your darts look, but don't compromise performance because of it.

The Flights

When it comes to flights, there are plenty of materials to choose from, like regular plastic, hard poly, real feather (usually turkey), or nylon. Personally, I don't worry about flights anymore. I rarely change mine more than two or three times a year.

What's the big secret? Nylon flights. I used regular plastic flights for years because I found a style that made my red darts look pretty flashy. Good looking, yes, but these flights weren't very durable and I found I was changing them every night (sometimes more) before I got sensible about it.

I know, I know, nylon flights don't normally come decorated with your favorite saying (i.e., "Dart Bitch") or have your favorite, topless Playboy bunny on them, but you can get nylons in a variety of different colors which should suit your set just fine, considering you aren't throwing away all that good money anymore.

Next, let's talk about the shape of your flights. While there are about a dozen popular shapes, you'll notice many of the better players tend to stay away from the larger, "butterfly" shaped flights. Sure, they produce enough drag on a dart to straighten out even the worst corkscrew throws (something better players don't have to worry about anyway), but they're just too big for an incoming dart to get around when you're trying to group three in a triple bed, or execute a critical hat trick. In this situation, a dart coming in on top of one already stuck in the board has a much greater potential for getting thrown out of an intended target by these huge obstructions. For me, they quickly proved to be a waste of my better efforts at the line.

If you absolutely can't live without butterfly flights, get yourself a high quality "spinner" shaft that doesn't rattle. These will help move the flight out of the way of other, incoming darts. They also work pretty well in making regular plastic and hard poly flights last longer, too. However, be warned that you should pack plenty of spare shafts, as spinners tend to break at the worst of times!

My opinion – and it's a popular one – is to get your set fitted with the "coal cracker" or, at most, the "fantail" shaped flights. Find these shapes in nylon, and you've got a long lasting, zero-headache flight for your darts.

The Flight Protector

For soft-tip players, the flight protector is a piece of "jewelry" that is a complete waste of time and money. (Aren't you glad I'm not opinionated about some things?) This aluminum fitting sits at the top of the flight and comes in a variety of pretty, metallic colors.

In its defense, however, there is a legitimate reason why this product was developed. Its roots began with steel-tip players attempting to minimize what is known as the "Robin Hood effect," where an incoming dart splits and sticks in the back of a dart's flight that is already in the board. This typically occurs when the cross-section's glue at the top of the flight splits from age and abuse, leaving an entry point for an incoming dart.

While the "Robin Hood" accuracy might look impressive, technically – in steel-tip – this second dart never made it to the board and does not get counted. However, to prevent this from happening in soft-tip play is nearly – excuse the pun – pointless, since the impact on the first dart already stuck in the board will register more of the same score.

My irritation with the flight protector is that they are too likely an item to pop off a dart and get lost. Once, I had a darts match delayed while I watched three people crawling on their hands and knees trying to find one of these tiny aluminum nuisances! And guess what? It came off again later, too! While it's a pretty accessory, don't waste your time or money with this product.

The Shaft

First and foremost, if you're using a metal shaft, get yourself a set of "O" rings. These are tiny washers that keep your barrel and shaft from rattling apart after every throw at the board (polycarbonate shafts don't need them). If you throw without them you already understand what a nuisance it is to constantly retighten your shaft and barrel together each time you pull them from the board.

There are plenty of materials out there to choose from for dart shafts, like hard polycarbonate, steel wire, or aluminum (spinners or non). Personally, I like the performance of the polycarbonate shaft, as they will remain straight even after hitting the floor repeatedly, unlike most metal shafts.

Typically, the polycarbonate shaft works best with a metal spring (see the book cover for an example), which slips on before loading the flight so each of the shaft's prongs remain tight and secure around the flight. With the spring, it's still possible for the flight to come off, but it won't happen nearly as often as it would without the spring.

Next, let's examine the length of the shaft. Shafts that are too short for you cannot help stabilize a dart in mid-flight as it travels to the target. Your throw and release must be near perfect to attain any accuracy with the shortest ones on the market. This is not recommended for beginners.

Shafts that are too long, on the other hand, provide plenty of stability in the air, but can be problematic for the second or third incoming darts in the same target. This problem is a bit similar to what we saw with large flights. Remember, the longer the dart that is stuck in the board, the greater the potential those that follow will get knocked further away from an intended target.

See the chapter titled, "This and That" for ways to extend the life of your polycarbonate shafts.

Tips

Finally, I recommend you get yourself a batch of 2Ba sized Tufflex II or III tips from your darts supply reseller. Actually, I can't remember seeing a tungsten dart that *didn't* use the 2Ba size. While there are a wide variety of tips to choose from, I can testify these will last all day in a long tournament with only a moderate amount of reshaping needed when they get bent. My experience with them is that they will rarely break. That's impressive.

My wife and I used to buy cheaper tips in quantities of 1000. It wasn't uncommon for us to change them out more then once a night. Therefore, a bag of 1000 would only last us about six or seven months. My experience with the Tufflex tips, though, is that this quantity would last us between two and three times longer.

Bottom Line: While buying darts is a completely individual thing, you'll likely be happiest with 2Ba tungsten barrels, medium-length polycarbonate shafts with flight-grip springs (remember, no "o-rings" needed for polycarbonate shafts), Tufflex tips, and nylon coal-cracker-styled flights. Be sure to pack spares of everything replaceable before you travel to your darting events. Flights, springs, tips, and shafts seem determined to break or pop off and disappear in some dark corner of the bar at the most inopportune of times.

Practice, Practice, Practice!

"Success is the sum of small efforts, repeated day in and day out..."
~ **Robert J. Collier**

Note: Since the bottom line of "practice" is to improve your general level of play, some of what I describe in this chapter will deal with challenges to improve your game *while* you play in your leagues and tournaments, too, not just through solitary training. Our focus when we discuss practicing is to help you keep things interesting long enough for the underlying basics to take root and improve your game overall.

Getting Really Basic

First, let's cover some basic points that might be obvious to most darters. However, for the purposes of this book, newer players might benefit from some clarifications.

When I refer to "'01" games in this book, I'm talking about the count-down games of 301, 501, 701, 901, etc., where a score of zero wins. Technically, it's all the same game, so for our purposes here I will refer to them all as '01, unless there is a need to get more specific, like 501 DI/DO (I'll explain "DI" and "DO" later on).

Next, the targets: The Bull's Eye, of course, is in the center of the board. In soft and steel-tip you will often hear it referred to as a "split Bull" because it is really two targets. Unlike steel-tip, though, '01 games in soft-tip will typically count both of these as 50 points. (Soft-tip "Cricket" games give only the very middle portion 50 points after the Bull's Eye has been "closed" and is able to generate points, provided an opponent has not closed that number, yet. The surrounding area – again, in Cricket – is worth 25 points.)

Single-valued targets immediately surround the Bull's Eye, and beyond these (moving outward) you'll find a ring that is triple the value of the number you see at the edge of the board. For instance, looking at the 17, hitting this segment on the triple ring will – doing the math – give you 51 points. Become familiar with your triples, along with their values, and practice them often. Pay particular attention during your practices to the targets of T20 through T15, as these are critically important in Cricket.

Moving outward beyond the triples are more single-valued targets and, finally, the outer ring is worth double the number you see at the edge of the board. Your doubles are important in '01 games, but are significant in Cricket, as well. Become familiar with these targets, especially the D20 (a double 20) through D12 where the values are 40 through 24, as these are what I call "soft-shouldered" targets in '01. We'll discuss the importance of these later in a section of this chapter called, "71."

The Warm-Up

I have a few stretches I like to employ before playing in order to loosen up my shoulder, forearm, and fingers, instead of waiting to get a few games deep into a match before the kinks get worked out. In this regard, being proactive and doing a few quick stretches seems to help my averages quite a bit. I find my overall mechanics – from the shoulder down – are much smoother and steadier.

For my shoulder, I'll do a few slow "windmills" to rotate and stretch the tendons and muscles around the joint. Next, I'll point my elbow back and upward toward the ceiling for a few moments to really focus on stretching the muscles at the front of the shoulder, which is essential for my arm's stability during the throw.

For my wrist and forearm, I like to make a hard fist and slowly work the entire wrist joint in a circular motion. With this, you should feel the muscles on the top and bottom of the forearm contract or stretch, dependent on the position of your fist.

Finally – and be careful with this next one – to stretch my throwing hand, I'll place the fingers of my right hand in the palm of my left hand and slowly pull them backward over my wrist. You can really feel a good stretch from your fingers, through the palm of your hand, to the underside of your wrist and forearm with this exercise. Hold it for a few moments before release, but remember, don't overstrain them.

Having done all these stretches, you should be loose and ready to go.

A Practice Space at Home

Regarding practice, I might suggest – instead of frequenting your favorite bar night after night – you buy a board for your home or garage where the drinks are cheaper and you can work out any issues with your game in peace. Making changes to how we throw can take time and focus. Use these times productively to iron out the bugs.

Second, if there is something unfinished around the house that threatens to preoccupy your thoughts as you practice – simply put – don't practice. Take care of whatever it is that's on your mind first. A half-hour spent in undistracted, focused practice beats hours of throwing where your mind is preoccupied on other issues.

Finally, do not get too comfortable practicing at home. Many players become the greatest throwers their basement's have ever seen, but leaving those cozy confines to play in the real world proves to be another matter completely. Often, these players are rattled when they play in a bar by a number of factors outside their control. Music, lighting, foot traffic around the throwing area, and general bar noise are among these.

Be sure you play outside your own comfortable practice area often.

Practice Routines

One of my favorite practice routines consists of fourteen count-up games (also called "high score"), where each game is spent throwing at a single target:

Game #1)	Bull's Eye
Game #2)	D20 (or "DTop")
Game #3)	D18
Game #4)	D15
Game #5)	D17
Game #6)	D19
Game #7)	D16
Game #8)	T20
Game #9)	T18
Game #10)	T15
Game #11)	T17
Game #12)	T19
Game #13)	T16
Game #14)	Bull's Eye

Notice this routine starts and ends with a Bull's Eye, but otherwise works from the top of the board, clockwise, to the bottom-left. This will help you develop your "range" on these bigger targets, instead of jumping from one end of the board to the other. While jumping about to various targets might be realistic during the course of a game, this exercise will give you a feel for targets in relation to one another. The differences between a harder effort at T18, a softer, lower effort at T15, and the "in between" effort to the Bull's Eye should become very apparent through utilizing this routine.

If your board goes ten rounds for count-up, these 14 games will give you 420 throws worth of practice at these various targets. With this, you can strengthen your accuracy on the biggest '01 important doubles, the biggest Cricket-important triples, and the always-critical Bull's Eye.

But be flexible with your practicing, too. While it's not a particular benefit to adopt one practice routine, you will want a standard to return to in order to gauge your development.

For example, if I notice I'm not as accurate with a particular target, especially the Bull's Eye, I'll give it some extra attention. In addition to the routine above, I like to spend some time on the doubles of 14 and 12, too, for their importance in '01 (12 is the lowest "soft-shouldered" double on the board ... more later). Regardless of the target, newer players should make a goal of 600 points each for these 14 games if their board goes ten rounds in count-up (480 points, obviously, for eight round boards).

A Word About the "Dreaded 16"

Cricket is a right-dominant game, meaning all targets are either situated centrally or right on the board. Only the 19 (barely) and 16 are to the left. It is not uncommon, then, for some right-handed players to have a problem making adjustments for throwing to their left.

While the 19 might be of little concern since it lays only one "pie slice" off of center, it's the 16 that is so problematic to many. The reason: a throw to the left is longer for right-handed players who typically don't move on the line much and maintain a more centralized stance to the board. Unless you're willing to change your position to this target, the 16 – deceptively so – requires a bit more muscle behind the dart and/or a greater arc to the throw.

As a right-handed player, I have improved my successes with the 16 when I turn my foot completely parallel to the line (as opposed to keeping my toes pointing toward the eleven o'clock position). At this angle, if there were a wall to the left of the throw lane, my right toes would be pointing directly at it.

If 16 is a problem for you, give this stance a try. My own successes with it were – in quick order – rather dramatic. Spend a count-up game throwing with your old stance at the 16, and one in this new way. If you scored a similar amount of points with the new method, remember that's pretty impressive for your first time. Keep at it. It might feel uncomfortable at first, but making the 16 a strength instead of a weakness should be motivation enough for you to embrace it.

Practicing with Steel-Tip Boards

If you merely want some target practice and have no need for an electronic scorekeeper, I would suggest maintaining the standard, eight-foot throwing distance for soft-tip boards, but use a steel-tip board, instead. Be sure to buy steel-tip conversion points for your soft-tip darts, too. They'll screw into your barrel just like regular soft-tips. You may also want to add O-Rings to these, but this is a minor preference, since there is considerably less jarring (and subsequent loosening) between your points and barrels as they enter these boards ... unless you hit a wire.

Why practice with a steel-tip board? For one thing, the targets are smaller, and your level of accuracy will transfer nicely to an electronic board's larger targets.

These boards will also illustrate problems with your throw, as your darts will stick at a variety of angles if you have an incorrect release. Your goal when it comes to sticking your darts in a steel-tip board is to drive them straight in. Don't be satisfied if they're angled (flights up or down), like some steel-tip pros do it. Some steel-tippers do this to get a cleaner look at a target they intend to revisit that round. Sticking a dart straight into the board will help you avoid nuisance bounce outs when you move back to a regular soft-tip board.

An important note about steel-tip boards: If you frequent a bar that has a steel-tip board, *do not throw your soft-tipped darts* *at it.* Why? Soft-tip points are shorter and much too blunt. On a steel-tip board – if a soft-tip dart is going to stick – the dart must be thrown a bit harder, which means it will burrow deeper into the board and, when removed, leave a loose gap behind. Steel-tip players have a hard enough time struggling against lost scores when darts fall out of a *good* dartboard. Add the frustrations of using a board that won't hold their darts well in the sections you've damaged and one can begin to understand why they wouldn't be too happy. To avoid unnecessary conflict with our steel-tip brethren, use your steel-tip conversion points with your soft-tip darts when using any of their boards. These points cost approximately $2.50 a set, and will certainly save you some unnecessary confrontations.

Practicing with Electronic Dartboards

There are some electronic boards with smaller, steel-tip sized targets, too, and they can cost as much as a good bristle board ($30 and up). In particular, Halex has a battery driven model in this price range, but other manufacturers like SportCraft make them, also.

Personally, I purchased a used, standard sized, Valley Cougar board from a local amusement company. I would strongly suggest investigating used boards from a local amusement vendor for two reasons: 1) if these models are sturdy enough to withstand bar room abuse, they are certainly sturdy enough for your home, and; 2) upon purchase, you've now done business with a local, knowledgeable vendor who can make a "house call" to repair it when servicing is needed.

One of the features that made my dartboard purchase an easy one was the onboard computer opponent, "Honest Ernie." While there is no substitute for shooting against a real opponent, Ernie is a great alternative. Many electronic boards today have a feature like this. I would suggest spending the few extra bucks to get one.

Cricket and the Computer Opponent

When playing the computer in a game of Cricket, dial its skill level all the way to the top. Why? It makes no sense to have the benefit of a world-class Cricket opponent in your own basement or garage and *not* take advantage of playing against it regularly. Starting out at a low skill level and gradually working your way up is a waste of your better practice efforts. Turn it up to "11" and face the fact you're going to get your butt whipped. Your drive to beat the computer at this level will really develop and shape your game.

Practice correctly, though. When it looks as though the computer's next round will be the last of the game, do not start closing various numbers around the board simply to improve your average before the game ends! You wouldn't play against a real opponent this way (if you want to pull a win out of the ashes), so do not practice this way, either. Continue to close and point appropriately.

To make sure your practice sessions remain productive, you should keep a simple log of your averages for each game. Most electronic boards will provide your stats in marks per round (MPR) for Cricket, and points per dart (PPD) for '01 when the game is finished. For Cricket, just record them on a sheet of paper like this:

Cricket - Date: 02/07

	1.8 MPR	
√	2.4	
	2.3	
√	3.2	
√	3.4	
	0.8	
	2.6	
Average:	2.38	← *Add up your average MPR's and divide by the number of games.*

Place a checkmark next to those averages where you led on points, at least once, somewhere in the game, beyond the first round.

If you ever win a game against the computer's top level, be sure to place an asterisk next to that average. These will be very rare, but relish them when they occur.

'01 and the Computer Opponent

Use a similar log when practicing your '01 games in order to track your PPD. And, I would suggest you strengthen your skills by playing what the masters play ... 501 DI/DO ("DI/DO" stands for "double-in" and "double-out").

Also, make some changes to the computer's skill level in '01, too. Unlike Cricket – where over the course of several games you will likely shoot at every target – dial the skill level back on your '01 games enough so that, while you are still challenged, you also get to practice that winning clutch shot regularly enough. If you leave the computer's skill level at its highest, it's rare you will ever get the opportunity to practice your double-out finishers. Make certain the skill level is not too easy, though. You'll still want to maintain good, competitive pressure on yourself.

To measure what level really challenges you, start out at the lowest level and move up to where the computer beats you at least sixty percent of the time. At that point, you'll have adequate pressure and enough opportunities for you to win and (ultimately) master that skill level to move up.

The Best Practice

Without question, one of the best things you can do for your game is to compete against others in your darts community as often as possible. Period. This brings you face to face with real clutch shots, distractions you must work through, a throwing rhythm, and helps you develop better concentration skills as opposed to merely winning or losing against the computer in the safety and comfort of your own home.

The real reason why competition brings out the best in some of us is that we develop a certain reputation over the years in our darting circles. No one wants to get beaten horribly and have it talked about with other shooters whose respect we hope to earn or keep. You'd be amazed at how the most seemingly innocuous wins and losses (to the inexperienced) can spread like wildfire across your darting community's grapevine. Realize this occurs and use it as a motivational tool to keep you focused with every dart you throw.

For an important opinion on the best form of practice and competition, take a look at John Lowe's observation in the "This and That" chapter.

Learning to Deal with Distractions

One of the biggest problems I see with players who shoot most of their darts in a one-board tavern is the inability to focus at tournaments when there is so much going on around them. The problem begins for them when tournament officials set the boards up side-by-side, about three feet apart (this distance will vary according to the space available for the tournament area), resembling a "shooting gallery." When these players are at the line without shooters on either side of them, they're fine. But as soon as someone steps into their field of peripheral vision, their round begins to fall apart.

Darts players should remember, first and foremost, this is not bowling. Whatever courtesies are applied in the bowling alley when people are preparing to bowl in the next lane are, or should be, non-existent in darts. The reason: If each of a thousand shooters in the bigger tournaments were to do this, day tournaments would last a week. Learn to shoot with other players next to you, especially those to the left if you're a right-handed player, and vice-versa for lefties.

Overcoming distractions at the line like this are one of the bigger detriments to shooting alone at home or in a one-board tavern. You can work out the intricacies of many things during these private practice sessions, but you can't add the unexpected distractions you must make yourself learn to ignore. Make it a point to play in all types of environments, especially if there is one that distracts you the most.

Personally, while I have a great fondness for this particular tavern, the most difficult board in any of my leagues or tournament sites is board #1 at The Curve Inn in Springfield, IL. Here's why: the board sits on a short wall where there's an open doorway left of it to another room. In that room is a single dartboard (within sight, anyway), and a pool table. In this example, I'm not simply trying to rule out distractions occurring next to me, peripherally. The distractions I'm referring to are occurring left of the board itself. Too much traffic in that room while I'm at the line and I begin to lose my focus for the job – and my intended targets – before me. However, since I realize I have problems with this board, I try to practice on it as much as possible. Honestly, I expect it will be a "non-issue" in the coming months and will ultimately make me a tougher opponent. I mention it here only to illustrate common distractions each of us must continually work on to overcome.

As much as you may not enjoy it at first, set your mind to shooting in multi-board darts taverns and tournaments whenever you get the chance. After awhile, a good player won't give it a second thought.

"71"
To practice my '01, clutch setups and double-outs, I've been playing the short game of 71 lately. The object is to pretend you have 71 points remaining in a game, while trying to set yourself up for a double-out, ideally, in two darts. Using more then three darts to take out this score results in a loss.

To play, setup a count-up game on your electronic board. The goal is to score 71 points every round, with a double-out finish. With your first dart, you'll want to even up this odd number by hitting a triple value, like 33, 39, or 45, and then nail the potential double-out value of 38, 32, or 26 with your remaining dart in that same round. Remember, it's a one round game, so you can see each of these will go very quickly. Keep a log of your wins and losses to get a good feel for how these practices are going.

To take out a 71, my favorite method is to shoot the first dart at a T13 for 39 points, which leaves 32. Nailing this target leaves you with the soft-shouldered D16. I refer to numbers like this as "soft-shouldered" because a miss on either side of the D16 will not bust you in a game of '01. In fact, remember all doubles on the dartboard are "soft" when counting backward from 20 to 12. While pros endeavor to leave nothing less then 32 points to double-out, I would suggest newer players strive for nothing less than 24 points.

Whenever you win, give yourself a "W." If you only used two darts, you should also give yourself a checkmark next to that win on your log sheet. Your 71 log, simply enough, should look something like this:

71 - Date: 02/09/05

	W
√	W
	L
√	W
	L
	W
	L
	L
	W
	W

The $1 Entry Fee

Real competition drives us like nothing else. Now, want to add some extra pressure to your games? Play against others for a buck.

While I don't advocate gambling, at these low-dollar wagers let's just call them "entry fees" and get past all the ugly connotations. We generally don't have a problem paying $5 to enter a tournament for a chance to place in the money, so why not view this as a "mini" tournament where winner takes all? It is simply another way to lend your practices some new intensity.

Using this as a tool, I've watched some average shooters ultimately become some of the best players my city has to offer just because they became unaffected by the added pressure money brings to these games. All told, when it comes down to it, they likely broke even after so many years, but were able to take their game to the next level in the process.

You could even make a challenge like this on the side during your league play with an opponent or a teammate. Don't be afraid to spice up the routine a bit and learn to enjoy these challenges.

Penny-A-Point

Another good practice challenge is to shoot a count up game for a penny-a-point, where the losers pay the winner a penny for every point difference between their scores and his.

This is an interesting challenge, especially when there's a good shooter in the mix. You'll be surprised at how well B-rated players step up against better opponents when the amount at stake is unclear at the outset.

The "DOH!" Darts Team Fund

During league play, another motivating way to help the entire team improve their averages is to pay into a "DOH!" fund each time a player doesn't achieve a minimum feat. For example, in Cricket, teams who employ this challenge typically require the shooter to pay a quarter each round where he fails to hit a two-mark minimum (forgiving the one-dart win, of course).

You may also consider giving a quarter back to a player every time they have a big round like a seven, eight, nine mark, or a hat trick.

Trust me, this idea is a winner. Why? This method makes a player focus on *every* dart, not just the game as a whole.

I've just recently witnessed a friend and his teammates improve, on average, nearly half a mark per round in one season (this is huge), and you wouldn't believe the amount of money they had when the league was over! If you're interested in introducing this to your team, have a test run on paper first to initiate the idea and let everyone "feel out" the added expense of it.

With the money collected during the season, you could meet up between leagues and have a team practice party completely paid for, or even pay the league fees of the entire next season for the whole team!

Some things to consider before adopting this idea: First, you'll need to appoint someone honest, responsible, and who rarely misses league night to organize this for the team. You may even want to have this person tally each "DOH!" in a log so everyone can see who paid the least at the end of the season, and who paid the most.

This will work with '01 leagues, also. My master's partner and I have been struggling the last few seasons, so we've recently added the "DOH!" fund to our league play. The rules on what constitutes a "DOH!" are a bit more advanced for our needs,

Soft-Tip Darts for the New Player: A Quiver of 3

but you could adapt the following to fit a regular '01 league, too (or combine it with the 2-mark minimum method for Cricket, if your league shoots both in one night).

Here's what our 501 DI/DO masters log looks like:

```
Date: ___/___/___              Opponent: _____

Home: 0         Away: 0

                           Tim                    Nate
Under 50 pts. - 25¢        0000 0000 0000         0000 0000 0000
                           0000 0000 0000         0000 0000 0000
                           0000 0000 0000         0000 0000 0000

Not In, 1st Rnd - 25¢      0000 0000 0000         0000 0000 0000
Not In, 2nd Rnd - 50¢      0000 0000 0000         0000 0000 0000
Not In, 3rd Rnd - 75¢      0000 0000 0000         0000 0000 0000

Missed Out - 25¢           0000 0000 0000         0000 0000 0000

Bust - 25¢                 0000 0000 0000         0000 0000 0000

A) Subtotal                $_____         $_____

Hat Trick / High Ton
Credit - 25¢               0000 0000 0000         0000 0000 0000

B) This Week's Totals: $_____             $_____

C) Last Week's
Season Totals:             $_____         $_____

D) New
Season Totals:             $_____         $_____
- Copy results of Items D to Items C for the next week. -

Rules:
Doesn't get in, 1st round - 25¢
Doesn't get in, 2nd round - 50¢
Doesn't get in, 3rd round and after - 75¢
Gets in, but under 50 pts. thrown in a round - 25¢
Under 50 pts. thrown in a round - 25¢
Any bust - 25¢
Board is under 50 pts., but frozen - No payment
Misses winning dart out opportunity - 25¢
Misses winning dart out opportunity and busts - 25¢ + 25¢
Credit for hat tricks and high tons - 25¢
```

We like the idea of having a record of what we've done all in one place, which includes information like who we shot against, the date, or whether we were "home" or "away." For every "DOH!" we color in a circle, then tally up what we owe at the end of the night. Overall, this idea has been a winner for us, too. Give it a try!

Developing Your Darts Math Skills

"Given the pace of technology, I propose we leave math to the machines and go play outside."
~ **Calvin & Hobbs**

Not being able to count-out in '01 is a popular weakness with newer players. Taking out a large number is something that typically gets "beaten" into a shooter over time, but it doesn't have to be that way. There is a simple math trick you can employ to quickly overcome these large, intimidating numbers.

Here it is: If you have a remaining score of, say, 143 and you want to see what will happen to your score if you threw a 57 (T19), simply round up the 57 to 60 points, do the subtraction, then add those 3 points back to the end result. Understand? It would look like this on paper:

```
    143
    -60
   ----------
     83
     +3
   ----------
     86
```

Also, and this is important for the beginner, you should never wait until you are standing at the line to start figuring your outs. If you are at or under 180 points, once you pull your darts from the board (160 points if it's a double-out game), you should begin to focus on your winning combination of targets for the next round immediately. Do *not* go back to the bar and order a drink. Do *not* start talking to your partner about the train wreck you witnessed last weekend, and do *not* piddle your time away by flirting with that guy or girl seated across the room.

I think you understand my intent here. Start doing the math as soon as you return from the board ... even if you are certain you will be frozen by the time you throw again! Use these occasions as an opportunity to build faster, stronger math skills. Once you have mapped out your targets needed for a win, reward yourself with a drink, conversation or, um, flirting as you see fit. 'Nuff said.

On the other hand, to check for a "math shortcoming" in an opponent (a potential weakness for you to exploit), watch what they are attempting to hit with the *first* dart during a difficult, potential out. Is the number they were shooting at a part of the combination needed to win the game?

For example, you can win an '01 game with 153 points remaining in a few different ways, but shooting the first dart at the Bull's Eye in this round should either tell you a player is not capable of counting his way out where larger scores are involved, or he lacks confidence in his own ability. More often, if you're slightly behind, this weakness could provide an extra round for you to win the game ... providing *you* know what to shoot for.

If you can teach yourself to count-out sooner in your darting career, you'll have a tremendous advantage over other players who might struggle years to master these simple math skills. Some players just don't understand working with numbers like this. Admittedly, I've encountered shooters who couldn't count to save their lives, but were horribly accurate on the Bull's Eye. By the time they had their score down to a number they could manage mentally, my only hope to win was with a big round, which made it all the more important for me to know how to do it.

Even if your level of skill is not strong enough to nail these big combinations and win a game, making the attempt will always make you a stronger player, faster. If you miss your intended target with the first dart and can't cap the game with the remaining two darts, return to the Bull's Eye to get your score down as quickly as possible. When shooting with a partner in league play, this is critical to help keep you from "freezing" him out of a win (more about the Freeze Rule in the "Winning Strategies" chapter).

To learn '01 outs, you can start by taking a sheet of paper and figuring the needed throws with every number starting at 21 through 180. Of course, you'll want to figure as few darts to throw as possible. For example, 42 is a one dart out, while 43 and 44 are two. Understand?

Also, you will be a stronger player if you try to leave yourself a soft-shouldered out, which is any double target between the scores of 40 and 24 (D20 through D12, as mentioned in the "71" section of the previous chapter).

For odd-numbered scores of 147 or greater where you are attempting to double-out, always dismiss the attempt at the T15 from the list of options with the first or second dart. You'll need a T17 or T19, instead.

And, do not be intimidated by a large, remaining score. Go for it! From my own experience in this game, few things are more invigorating then nailing a big, accurate combination to steal a win.

Learning Your Outs

When reviewing out charts, remember there is a difference between steel-tip and soft-tip with regard to the more successful ways of winning a game. If you find a chart on the web, remember – unless they say otherwise – they are most likely geared toward the steel-tip community. If you were to buy an "out card" from your darts distributor, the gold-colored one is typically for steel-tip, whereas platinum (silver) is for soft-tip.

Why are there generally recognized differences in outs between steel-tip and soft-tip? First, aside from all targets being larger in soft-tip, the Bull is usually not split for '01 games. In steel-tip, the Bull is always split (the very middle equals 50, and the outer section equals 25).

Therefore, the success potential of using the Bull's Eye's large real estate for 50 points during a soft-tip game is just too great to ignore. There is simply much more of a target to utilize there. Many of the high out-combinations in steel-tip rely heavily on the oft-thrown (and therefore oft-practiced) T20. Soft-tippers tend not to rely on this smaller target so much in '01 games. Instead, we seem more then happy to sacrifice those extra ten possible points to throw at a bigger, central target we're more likely to hit.

At the end of this chapter, you'll find an '01 out-chart I have developed for soft-tip play. Admittedly, it is not perfect, as there is great debate (even among the pros) on how one should take out a game.

Let me give you two examples: John Lowe's perfect 501 game (the first before TV cameras) in 1984 went like this:

ROUND ONE	ROUND TWO	ROUND THREE
T20	T20	T17
T20	T20	T18
T20	T20	D18

On the other hand, in 1990, Paul Lim's (Medalist Grand Master Singles – 6 time champion; Singapore Open – 5 time champion;

Malaysian Open – 5 time champion; Asian Cup Singles – 5 time champion) televised, perfect, 501 game went like this:

ROUND ONE	ROUND TWO	ROUND THREE
T20	T20	T20
T20	T20	T19
T20	T20	D12

Who would dare argue with either of these two legendary players about which method is the correct one?

To shed some light on "why" these debates happen, the focus is mostly on the possibility of an inaccurate throw in a neighboring triple bed while attempting to win in as few extra darts as possible.

For instance, to win a game, a player might opt for shooting first at a T16 – instead of a T18 – to help win a game. The reason for this is that they may want to prepare for the possibility of accidentally hitting a neighboring triple around the T16 – either T8 or T7 – which might still leave them with an opportunity to win in that round, as opposed to hitting a T1 or T4 when shooting at the T18. But, trust me, when you start thinking like this there are enough combinations to make your head spin!

The Mystery of the D16

When you watch masters-level matches, have you ever wondered why so many shooters – especially the pros – prefer to double-in *and* double-out on the D16?

Well, here's the answer: The D16 is utilized significantly more often in successful out-combinations then any other target on the board. And, since the D16 is already an option they are very familiar with to *finish* a game, it only makes sense it is a popular target to *start* a game, too. Since you can't begin to "count down" in a masters '01 game until you successfully double-in, it's a simple case of "go with what you know." After all, familiarity breeds comfort, comfort breeds confidence, and confidence breeds victories. There you have it. Mystery solved!

The Soft-Tip Out Chart

Below you'll find a soft-tip out chart, based on an unsplit Bull's Eye.

This chart does not always take into account the possibilities of "if you miss your first triple, but land in a neighboring triple, you still have an opportunity to win with your remaining two darts." Although I consider myself a dart geek (proven by the fact I wrote a book on this topic), I'm just not *that* big a dart geek. In ten years, perhaps I'll write a follow-up for the intermediate player that further explores these combinations ... but not today.

For now, newer players should be satisfied with returning to the Bull's Eye to harvest big points if they miss a big triple with their first or second darts in order to get their scores down fast and not freeze their partners.

Soft-Tip Darts for the New Player: A Quiver of 3

180 - T20, T20, T20
179 - None
178 - None
177 - T20, T20, T19
176 - None
175 - None
174 - T20, T19, T19
173 - None
172 - None
171 - T19, T19, T19
170 - T20, T20, B
169 - None
168 - T19, T19, T18
167 - T20, T19, B
166 - None
165 - T19, T18, T18
164 - T20, T18, B
163 - None
162 - T18, T18, T18
161 - T20, T17, B
160 - B, B, T20
159 - T19, T20, T14
158 - B, T20, T16
157 - B, B, T19
156 - T20, T20, D18
155 - B, T20, T15
154 - B, B, T18
153 - T19, T20, D18
152 - B, T20, T14
151 - B, B, T17
150 - B, B, B
149 - T20, T19, D16
148 - B, B, T16
147 - B, T19, D20
146 - B, T20, D18

145 - T15, B, B
144 - B, T18, D20
143 - B, T19, D18
142 - B, B, T14
141 - B, T17, D20
140 - B, B, D20
139 - B, B, T13
138 - B, B, D19
137 - B, T17, D18
136 - B, B, D18
135 - B, T15, D20
134 - B, B, D17
133 - B, B, T11
132 - B, B, D16
131 - B, T15, D18
130 - B, B, D15
129 - B, T19, D11
128 - B, B, D14
127 - B, T19, 20
126 - B, B, D13
125 - B, T15, D15
124 - B, B, D12
123 - B, T19, D8
122 - B, B, D11
121 - B, T17, D10
120 - B, 20, B
119 - B, 19, B
118 - B, 18, B
117 - B, 17, B
116 - B, 16, B
115 - B, 15, B
114 - B, 14, B
113 - B, 13, B
112 - B, 12, B
111 - B, 11, B

110 - T20, B
109 - B, 9, B
108 - B, 8, B
107 - T19, B
106 - B, 6, B
105 - T20, T15
104 - T18, B
103 - B, 3, B
102 - B, 2, B
101 - B, T17
100 - B, B
99 - B, 17, D16
98 - B, T16
97 - T19, D20
96 - T20, D18
95 - B, T15
94 - T20, D17
93 - T19, D18
92 - B, T14
91 - T17, D20
90 - B, D20
89 - B, T13
88 - B, D19
87 - T17, D18
86 - B, D18
85 - T15, D20
84 - B, D17
83 - B, T11
82 - B, D16
81 - T15, D18
80 - B, D15
79 - T13, D20
78 - B, D14
77 - T19, D10
76 - B, D13

75 - T15, D15
74 - B, D12
73 - T19, D8
72 - B, D11
71 - 20, T17
70 - 20, B
69 - 19, B
68 - 18, B
67 - 17, B
66 - 16, B
65 - 15, B
64 - 14, B
63 - 13, B
62 - 12, B
61 - 11, B
60 - T20
59 - 9, B
58 - 8, B
57 - T19
56 - 16, D20
55 - 5, B
54 - T18
53 - 3, B
52 - 2, B
51 - T17
50 - B
49 - 17, D16
48 - T16
47 - 15, D16
46 - 14, D16
45 - T15
44 - 12, D16
43 - 11, D16
42 - T14
41 - 9, D16

Good Mechanics for Success

"I cannot say whether things will get better if we change. What I can say is they must change if they are to get better."
~ G. C. Lichtenberg

The Grip

This topic alone should – in equal numbers – send my fellow dartsmen off in a mad dash for the phone to chew me out or sing my praises. Here's the issue: how you grip a dart is a trade-off between two things – control and release. Between these two, there must be a balance, a happy medium.

The more fingers on a dart, the more control you have. Unfortunately, getting all five fingers *off* the dart evenly (a critical task) at the zenith of the throw is not always so easy, and can rob you of consistency.

Another troublesome method is the "pencil grip" throw, where you hold the dart as if you were going to write your name with its tip on a piece of paper. Unfortunately, while this grip provides excellent control, it is a grip best designed to *hold* something ... not let go of it. While Phil Taylor, who is arguably the greatest darts player to ever compete (World Champion: 1990, 1992, 1995, 1996, 1997, 1998, 1999, 2000, 2001, 2002, 2004, 2005), might employ the pencil grip throw, it's a bit difficult to master. His accolades and achievements aside, Taylor's preferred method might not be best suited for beginners.

Therefore, for those of you who are new enough to the sport, it's in your best interest to avoid these styles earlier in your darts career, as opposed to changing later on when it's more difficult.

A popular method, and one I feel is correct, is to use your thumb and index finger to hold the dart (thumb underneath and index finger on top, instead of them holding both sides of the dart), while using your middle finger (again, on top) to provide stability near where the tip meets the barrel.

Draw, Throw, and Release

First, hold the dart out in front of you at roughly eye level and size up your target. For right-handed players, your elbow should not be directly beneath your throwing hand, but in a more natural position slightly to the right.

As you hold the dart in front of you, keep it parallel to the floor. Draw back, then push forward, and release it at nearly the end of your arm's full extension, in one fluid motion. Remember not to jerk your arm forward when the draw is finished, as though it's a race to get the dart out of your hand and to the board. Keep the motion smooth as you pull back and then push forward. From start to finish the throw should be an unforced and controlled movement.

At the point of release, your elbow should have risen slightly (this helps create a slight arc in the darts trip to the board), while your index finger should be pointing at your target. Practicing this will help you with your follow through and eliminate the always too jerky, "snap" or "short arm" throw.

Draw the dart back to your forehead, nose, cheek, lips, chin, eye, temple, or ear. Whichever point you prefer makes little difference. Just avoid brushing the flight against any of them (your eye, in particular … ouch!) along the way.

Finally, focus on throwing the dart without a spin movement at the point of release. While it might feel natural to twist the dart in a clockwise motion (counter-clockwise for lefties) out of your hand as you let it fly, this will add yet another movement to the mechanics of your throw and robs consistency.

The "Push Throw"
As with anything in this sport, the draw itself can be a subject of debate among players. To give you an example, one of the better darts players in my community does not draw back at all, but starts with the flight next to his ear and begins his throw from that point in a method that is best described as a "push throw."

While not the most popular method of delivering a dart, there is no arguing with his successes with it, either. While difficult to master, it eliminates the draw completely and is one less movement to control, which I believe is always a positive.

If you can be patient enough to master this method, I would recommend it.

The "Push Grip"
It seems to me this particular discussion is more appropriate here (as opposed to above in the section titled, "The Grip") because a problem occurs – not when you first grasp the dart – but when the draw is completed, just before the beginning of the throw. At the end of the draw, the fingers bunch up, as though they are preparing – by themselves – to vault the dart toward the board once the arm fully extends. The index finger no longer has a slight arc pointed at the board but, instead, its fingertip is pointing straight down the palm. This is *not* correct!

I believe this mistake starts with players trying to add a bit of finesse to their throw. For myself, I have been guilty of employing this quirk for many years and, fortunately, recently dropped this bad habit with great benefit to my stats. It is likely I developed it by watching a player whose skill I admired (and still do) very much, adopting it unconsciously in the mid-to-late 1990s.

In a nutshell, this hand altering "push grip" is incorrect because – you guessed it – it adds another unnecessary movement to the throw. Avoid it, and let your arm do the work for you.

Your Stance
Your stance will evolve, too. If after 10 years it's the same as the first night you picked up a dart, you're a rare breed, indeed.

There are three typical throwing stances:

1) Your forward foot is parallel to the line;
2) The toes of your forward foot point to the ten or eleven o'clock position (one or two o'clock for you lefties), and;
3) The toes of both feet are at the throw line, each in the twelve o'clock position.

I would suggest throwing with each method described above and adopt the one that feels the most natural and comfortable for you.

The stance I employ at the moment resembles #1, except the heel of my back foot is not planted on the floor, as I believe it should be (this reduces body motion). While I endeavor to remain motionless during the throw, balancing solely on one foot can create a little unsteadiness at times. As I write this, I'm beginning to work with the "back foot flat on the floor" stance. I'm noticing in the process my level of accuracy improves as my body is easier to keep motionless, but I also notice I need more effort to get my darts to the board when I employ it. As I continue to marry this new stance into my game, I'll be curious to see how it affects my stats.

Economy of Motion
I've been mentioning it all along in this chapter, but it's important: Whichever throwing method you adopt, the crucial part of your mechanics is to limit all unnecessary movements.

Do not lift the heel of your forward foot, do not lift your back foot, and do not lunge forward in any way. Unnecessary body movements make throwing your darts with any consistency more difficult then it needs to be. The dartboard does not move, but if you practice the bad mechanics described here it may as well!

Consider the short distance to the board. You're throwing a dart less than eight feet, not a javelin for 150 yards. Keep your body still and just use your arm. For the new player, this may be difficult at first, but keep practicing.

Endeavor to remain motionless during each throw, *especially* with the third dart. I refer to the third dart specifically here for one reason: Typically, when lunging begins to take root in a player's mechanics, it will begin with the release of the third dart. Many darts players are guilty of beginning their step toward the board to retrieve them *while* the third dart is being thrown. The forward motion of the arm, the momentum following the release, and the lack of attention to good form all contribute to this. Without realizing it, I've seen darts players ultimately begin lunging with every throw.

If you tend to lunge forward during your throw, practice a longer, more flowing release while maintaining the muscular emphasis you used before. It will take a little practice, but better now then later after these bad mechanics have cemented themselves as a part of your throwing style.

For years I have played against one of the greatest darts players ever to come out of central Illinois. He is deadly accurate, but has a lunging habit that simply evolved after many years of play. He drifted into it so unconsciously over the years he's now perfected the timing of lunge and release during every throw. Today, if you were to ask him to remain still and throw a hat trick, I'm sure it would be like asking Elvis to sing and *not* gyrate on the Ed Sullivan Show in 1956.

Remember, our goal here is to highlight the straightest, clearest path for your success. Simply because a great player uses bad mechanics doesn't make the style one you should adopt. Unnecessary movement while you throw is contrary to the goal of improving your game as quickly as possible.

Booch Meets the Birdman
Probably the worst throwing mechanics I've ever seen happened in 1996 as I competed in the World Bullshooter event in Chicago, Illinois. During a match, I was paired against a most unusual opponent. He would balance on one foot, and hold his opposite leg stretched out behind him like a tail. With an extremely exaggerated forward lean, and his left arm held out like a wing from his body, he looked as though he were attempting to fly toward the board!

Add to this, the elbow of his throwing arm drew tiny, imaginary circles in the air as he prepared for every shot. Finally, after throwing a dart, he'd fall forward, only to reposition himself again in this wacky "birdman" position until all of his darts were spent. This poor guy teetered so awkwardly with every throw there was simply no way he could plant two darts in the same target. How he earned a first or second place finish to qualify for the tournament completely escapes me.

On the other hand (and, in hindsight, this might hold a clue as to how he qualified), I was so utterly distracted by this circus act I could barely muster a focus of my own. Fortunately for me, I won the match, no thanks to the bizarreness of it all.

How to Improve Control
There are a number of things we can do to improve control. Recently, I have come to realize (at the ripe old age of 42) I suffer from a slight case of tremors, although I cannot say with any certainty it is worse now then when I was 28. At any rate, it's not enough for me to go racing off to the doctor, but I have noticed it affecting my darts play on occasion (I'm pretty sure

caffeine plays a role here, too, but I'm not about to give up my Mountain Dew jones!).

The curious thing is, when I exercise my forearm lightly before league or tournament play, the tremors appear to diminish.

Currently, I use the Dynaflex Powerball hand, wrist, and forearm exerciser from Sharper Image. Using a gyroscope core and a ripcord to start its movement, the motion you use to keep it spinning is similar to opening a door where your wrist and forearm twist in unison. Add a slight rotation with your wrist to the combination of movements and you're on your way to a great forearm workout.

This is one of those products someone probably invented first as a novelty, and then realized later they were getting a pretty good hand and forearm workout, so that's how they marketed it. I'd be curious to see, though, how much more improvement I could get with an exerciser that employs individual resistance for each finger but – for the most part – I'm happy with my results with this.

While you wouldn't qualify me as having "Popeye forearms," I have noticed the greater the strength in my forearm, wrist, and fingers, the greater the control I have over my darts.

My point with highlighting my tremor issues is that it has led me to believe muscle development can help darts players a great deal. Do you want more power in your throw? Develop your triceps. Do you want greater control at your release? Exercise your fingers, wrists, and forearms. Do you want greater stamina for long tournaments? Focus on your legs, back, shoulders, and stomach.

And speaking of stomachs, do yourself a favor and keep a watchful eye on this area. Not only do the abdominal muscles help support our backs (reducing pain there), studies just out have suggested – on average – men with waists over 40 inches and women with waists over 35 inches are at greater risk for high blood pressure, diabetes, and heart disease. Knowing how much we love our beer and how much time we spend pursuing this sport of ours (eating "bar food" all the while), it's in all our best interests to keep a close eye – and work on – our midsections. 'Nuff said.

Bottom line: Hold the dart with the index and middle finger on top, with the thumb underneath. Your draw and throw should be one steady, fluid motion (if you elect to use the draw at all). Decide which stance you prefer, but keep everything solid, from your feet, ankles, and calves, to your hips and shoulders. The only thing in motion should be your throwing arm, and most of that should be from the elbow down.

The Power of Imagery

"The man who has no imagination has no wings."
~ **Muhammad Ali**

First, let's define the word "imagery" and how it can be used constructively. Imagery – in its simplest definition – is the process by which you can create, modify, or strengthen pathways important to the co-ordination of your muscles by using your imagination.

Huh?!?

Let me explain: To gain the full benefits of imagery you'll first need to completely relax in a comfortable chair and close your eyes. And turn off the TV, the radio, and any other audible distractions, too.

After some deep breaths, let's begin the relaxation process, starting with your toes. How do they feel? Are they curled inside your shoes, or are they straight and relaxed, with no muscles controlling them? Now, consciously move your attention to your ankles. Loosen them if they aren't that way already. Move to your calves in the same way, then up your legs. Each set of muscles should be free of any muscular controls you might unconsciously be placing on them. How about your hips? Are they relaxed as you sit there?

Do this throughout the rest of your body: fingers, wrists, elbows, flexors, extensors, biceps, triceps, shoulders, back, abdominals, neck, lips, cheeks, and forehead (meaning, don't "knit" your eyebrows as you try to concentrate on relaxing). I think you'll be amazed to find muscles you didn't even realize were taut when you started this relaxation process.

Now that your body is in a fully relaxed state, let's employ your imagination. Imagine yourself as you walk into a familiar bar where an opposing team of players awaits you. Imagine they are disappointed you are there, perhaps not realizing it was you they were shooting against that night. Imagine they've heard about you, or have played against you before, and they remember well the beating they took. Your arrival makes it painfully clear another loss is imminent, and they aren't happy about it.

You hear someone cuss in the room, then see a player from the opposing team drop his darts on a tabletop in frustration. You look at them and smile a knowing, cocky smile.

The room goes quiet as you remove your darts from your case and set about warming-up for the match. Stepping to the line, you throw a dart. Smack! Bull's Eye. Throwing your second one, you hear it rustle past the flight of the first dart already stuck in the board and ... POP! ... another Bull's Eye. Finally, the third dart makes it a hat trick. Play out all the details. From your stance, to your release, then the position of your hand as each dart flies to the board. Now, approach the board to remove your darts and notice you've grouped these so closely together that each dart's barrel is touching the other two.

Walking back to the line, darts in hand, you throw all three darts successfully into the T20, grouping them as before. You hear someone from the other team swear again in disbelief as you remove your darts from the board. In your mind's eye, turn and look at the opposing group again. A slight smirk crosses your lips as you turn back to the board. This is what confidence feels like. Relish it!

Continue in this manner for two more rounds before announcing you're ready. The match begins.

Whether the match is all Cricket, all '01, or a combination of these is not important. Just pick a game you need to work on and play out your perfect throws. You do not need to concern yourself with the successes or failures of your partner(s) or the opposition. Your perfect darts are guaranteed – in this exercise, at least – to win every game.

If you do this exercise correctly, it is completed in real time, meaning it should take you as long to shoot an imaginary match as it does a real one. This exercise requires focus, patience, and may even take time away from actually throwing real darts – but trust me – the results are worth it.

An Imagery Example

To help confirm imagery can really work for you, let me retell a true story, then you can judge for yourself whether it's an effective tool or not:

During the Vietnam War, Colonel George Hall was captured by the Viet Cong and held captive for seven years in a cage. During this time he was beaten and malnourished by his captors. Due to his rank, Hall was also kept apart from the other POWs for his potential to lead and organize an escape.

At first, he did little else but hope for his release. But as the weeks wore into months, Hall realized the boredom and isolation threatened to overwhelm him. Depression began to creep in, and he knew he had to find a way to occupy himself.

So, he began to focus on happier times. Ultimately, he began to concentrate on the one thing he loved to do most in the entire world: play golf.

Every day – using only his imagination – Hall went to one of his favorite golf courses and played 18 holes. He visualized the clothes he wore, listened to the trees rustle along the fairway, and admired the freshly mowed greens. He imagined various seasons and the weather they brought. Sometimes it was windy and springtime, or an overcast winter's day, or a hot summer's morning. He imagined them all.

In his mind, no detail of the course, from the grass, to the trees, to the singing birds, was left out. Squirrels and rabbits were commonplace along the fairways.

He could nearly feel the golf club in his hands, as he imagined the perfect stance, head down, the perfect swing. He heard the rush of the club, the pop of the ball, and the vibration from their contact in his hands as it traveled up the shaft. He saw the ball soar down the middle of the fairway, hop a few times, roll, then lie where he intended.

He took his time and enjoyed every single step. In this way, it took him just as long to play eighteen holes in his imagination as it would have taken in reality. He did this everyday for eighteen holes, smack down the middle of each fairway, with perfect green shots and putts, four hours a day, seven days a week, week in and week out for seven years. It was his only escape – if only for a short time every day – but he relished it.

Finally, the war ended and Hall was freed to return home. He'd gone through a great deal as a POW, and there was plenty of mending to do. But his friends and family rallied to him, helping out as his strength slowly returned.

As the days grew longer and warmer, his old golfing companions asked if he'd like to join them for a round at his favorite course. His eyes lit up at the thought. Golf had been so far from his mind once he came home, and now he realized it was an important part of the healing process for him to play again. He'd thought about it so much while he was imprisoned.

For the first time in over seven years he stepped onto a golf course and shot an unbelievable 74. Early on that day, his friends realized there was a huge difference in the Colonel's game since last they'd played. Amazingly, each ball – shot from the tee as though a cannon had fired it – went straight and true down the middle of each fairway. And if his green shots placed the ball any reasonable distance from the pin, his putts were nearly always dead on.

Once the last hole was played, the group gathered at the clubhouse and realized Hall had slashed 20 strokes off his handicap ... without having touched a golf club in over 2500 days! Instead of a 22-stroke handicap – like he had before his tour and imprisonment in North Vietnam – Hall was down to a stunning *two-stroke* handicap!

His friends were floored. They knew from his physical condition when he arrived home, from what Hall and his family had said of his imprisonment, and from the newspaper articles they'd read that this soldier suffered greatly as a POW. Surely, practicing golf while being held captive during wartime was a completely absurd notion based on these facts. Yet, how could Hall explain being away from the sport for so long, only to come back and shatter his personal best by twenty whole strokes?!

When asked about it, Hall tapped his head knowingly, smiled, and said: "To keep myself busy, I played 18 holes right here, everyday, for seven years."

Bottom line: While real practice is essential, imagery works because your brain still sends the same message along your neural pathways, the same as if you were physically completing each throw. The difference is you can make each throw in your imagination a perfect one. By imagining perfection you are teaching yourself how to throw your darts better and more correctly in the "real world." It's especially useful if you don't have access to a dartboard, and have some time to use the under realized powers of your imagination.

The Art of Confidence

"The first time I shot the hook I was in the fourth grade, and I was about five feet eight inches tall. I put the ball up and felt totally at ease with the shot. I was completely confident it would go in and I've been shooting it ever since."
~ **Kareem Abdul-Jabar**

Remember in your imagery exercises to practice confidence, too. Whether it's how you stand, how you walk, the darts you throw, the words you use, a knowing smile at your opponent – whatever method you can use to project this – confidence is the key to calming you down in tight situations. Confidence is what drives home Bull's Eye after Bull's Eye. Confidence lets you think clearly about how to win. Confidence relaxes you and allows your body to rise to the level of play required to beat the toughest opponents. Confidence is what separates the great players from the "also rans."

While we're on this topic, to those readers who feel the mental part of their darts game is lacking and would like some further guidance, I'm recommending "The Mental Edge," a book by Kenneth Baum. It's available at many bookstores, including Amazon.com This book is a great piece of work that has provided me with a lot of insight into areas like confidence, mental preparedness, and turning negative perceptions into positive ones. While it's not geared specifically toward darts players, it's written in an easy to understand style (as in, it's not strictly for high-minded, Mensa members!), and I believe it has a lot to offer people engaged in anything – and not just sports – where confidence and positive thinking can be used as effective tools. Baum and his co-author, Richard Turbo, have done a great job here. The book is riddled with real-life stories from athletes who've used Baum's ideas successfully and these, in particular, can be really inspiring. Be sure to read "Chapter Five: A Picture of Excellence."

I believe confidence is the key to winning. I would hazard to say that darts is 10% skill, 10% strategy, and 80% confidence. I've watched players who are deadly accurate when playing against most of the field, but when playing against a pro-level player they've never met before (and have only heard about), they don't feel worthy to stand at the line against them. Their performances bear this out. I've seen players who – by all rights – should win tournaments, but instead lose in crushing fashion at the end because they lost their confidence.

Now, I don't mean to speak of confidence as though it has an on/off switch. It does not. It is a cryptic creature, to be sure. The nature of confidence is hard to understand at times, and it takes real focus to attain and maintain.

You must *practice* being confident, just like you practice throwing darts. Any feelings of doubt, fear, or anxiety should be routed from your mind, just like your body's immune system would turn and attack a dangerous, intrusive virus. To be a confident darts player, you must *believe* you are a threat to the opposition every time you pick up a dart. In your mind, you know the other team dreads your every appearance at the line. You feel their hopes of winning wither away with every dart that leaves your hand. Your darts are weapons for you to punch out any combination of targets at will. No triple or double is too small for you. This is what confidence feels like. Make it a part of your game and preparation.

Spilled Milk

Next, there will be times when you are fully prepared, both mentally and physically, to play well. You arrived an hour early to warm-up before your match, you are relaxed, you have spent the better part of the day thinking about perfect throws and crushing opponents, but then you get to the line and have one critical, errant dart. Instead of shaking it off and focusing on your next throw or round, you berate yourself unmercifully.

It's true when people say, "You are your own worst enemy." With this self-criticism, you are tearing down your self-confidence unnecessarily, whether you realize it or not. And it's a real gift for the opposition, too. No one throws perfect darts, and no one expects you to do it, either. Letting go of mistakes is the only way to think clearly regarding future throws and winning.

When bad darts happen to good people (sorry, I couldn't resist) don't shake or hang your head in disgust. Don't let your inner voice cuss you out. Don't be negative regarding something you can't control any longer ... the event has already happened. It's done, over, finished. Beating yourself up too much is a disservice to yourself and your teammates. Shake it off and move on. If you need to take a short time-out to refocus, do it and give yourself a positive talking to, like this: "I am a good darts player. I will not be defined by one bad throw. If anyone here owns these targets, I do."

To some degree, everyone – at some point – will berate themselves. Some are simply more obvious (and distracting to themselves and their teammates) then others. Admittedly, this is an area where I need some extra work, too. My Irish/Italian temper has been known to get the better of me on more then one occasion. However, I have made it a point to strive harder to shrug errors off and keep my temper in check when things start going sour. After all, I still consider myself a "work in progress."

Bottom line: Everyone has the ability to exercise and flex his or her confidence "muscle." The better players in your community don't have to concern themselves with it too much, because they *believe* they have what it takes to win. You've got what it takes, too. Practice being confident.

A Tale From Inside "The Zone"

"I would have to say that such things seem to exist or emerge when your state of mind is right. It has happened to me dozens of times. An intention carries a force, a thought is connected with an energy that can stretch itself out in a pass play or a golf shot or a thirty-foot jump shot in basketball. I've experienced it too many times to deny its existence."
~ **John Brodie**

What is "the zone?" Well, it's a strange state of mind, to be sure. It is an impenetrable marriage of confidence, focus, will, ability, and strategy. When a player is inside "the zone," his darts feel great, his mind is clear and quick, his focus intense, and his aches and pains are meaningless.

The Tale

Two local shooters, Kenny Fitzgerald and Lynnie Neal, Jr., became world champions during the spring of 1995 at the Pro (Cricket) Doubles event of Bullshooter X. Later, in the fall of that year – with Kenny and Lynnie set to shoot in a Cricket league here in town – teams were forming fast as players came out of the woodwork to shoot with and measure themselves against these two recent world champs. As far as darts go, everyone would admit, Kenny and Lynnie's big win at Bullshooter infused a lot of life into the local darts scene.

Normally an '01 shooter, my participation in this Cricket league came about when acquaintances of mine – Larry and Chuck – began looking for two other guys to form a team. Dale (a longtime friend and '01 teammate of mine) was approached by them and agreed to shoot. When they asked if he knew anyone else who'd make a good fourth player, mentioning my name apparently raised Larry and Chuck's eyebrows a bit. Admittedly, I was pretty green when I last played against them in 1992.

So, Dale called me one night and asked if I'd be interested in joining up with them. Knowing the other guys a little, I told him it sounded like a good idea. However, I soon learned a mere acceptance on my part wasn't all that was required. Larry and Chuck would only agree to include me on the team if they could evaluate, first hand, how well I could throw.

Now, by 1995 I had developed my game pretty well, and had a good reputation as a solid player. My stats were posted – like everyone else's – on a bulletin board in most every darts bar in town. If these two didn't know me very well by then, they certainly knew the players around me on these sheets, and could make a fair assessment of my talent (or lack thereof). More then anything else, the underlying rub was that I had to audition for a spot on this team. Actually, for me, calling it a "rub" was a gross understatement.

Dale wisely allowed me – and the phone wires – to cool a bit as he explained the benefits of the venture. In the end, I decided to do it because: A) I knew Larry, Chuck, and Dale were good, capable players; B) Dale and I had become good friends; C) I'd never shot in a Cricket-only league before and wanted to, and; D) I, too, wanted to measure myself against Kenny and Lynnie. This appeared to be my only opportunity in the near future to do this, so I agreed to the audition.

A few nights later I arrived at the designated tavern and the three of us began shooting three-way Cricket. To say I was anxious to draw "first blood" would be sarcasm at its finest. In the days prior to our meeting, my thoughts were completely consumed with annihilating these two in every game. (Dale elected to stay home that night, as he jokingly told me he was pretty certain I'd "make the cut.")

The best description for what happened to me that night is this: When I stood at the line I was in a different place, almost like I was looking through someone else's eyes. I was somehow detached, yet also the center of everything.

I can remember the dartboard appeared monolithic to me, too, as though I was sitting in the front row of a movie theater looking up at a twenty-foot tall dartboard on the screen. Who could miss such huge targets? It was a strange state of mind for me, to be sure.

At the line I would slip into this "daze" more, then – as I walked away from the board – would surface a bit, but never too much. I also remember not being very talkative (a rare event, indeed).

Preparing to shoot, I remember the patron's voices in the bar along with the music from the jukebox seemed to blend together into a "white noise," becoming indiscernible and leaving me with zero distractions. At the line, a dart was in my hand one instant then, with very little effort, buried in my target the next. How it arrived there was completely fluid and effortless. I certainly didn't have to wrestle with any details involved with throwing. I just understood what I needed to do, and didn't fret over the details.

While Larry and Chuck are good players, I won every game that night, as each of us ran through about $15 worth of quarters. Seven and eight round games were not uncommon as I found myself blistering all targets effortlessly. I was so consumed with each throw I'm convinced they couldn't have won a single game, even with a bonus dart every round. If we'd have been opponents on a battlefield, history books today would remember that night as a "scorched earth" campaign. In my life, I have never pounded other players as hard as I did those two that night.

Since I kept winning, I was always slotted to shoot last in the next game. I can remember once, past the evening's halfway mark, I was so confident and "in the zone" I threw a "white horse (nine marks, three different triples, scoring no points)" in the first round. Not that remarkable by itself, but Larry and Chuck already had me down by 80 and 40 points, respectively. I can remember Larry was particularly pleased with himself after closing the 20 and pointing it so well. It was one of his best openings that night.

Now, not trying to stay close or ahead in points is normally pretty brainless when you are down by that much so early, but in my confident state of mind I waved off any apprehension surrounding the score. In that first round, I closed the 20, 19, and 18, instead of pounding triple 19s to make points. The score really meant nothing to me then. I was confident I would take care of it later.

Continuing, the other numbers fell almost as easily as these first three so, once I closed the Bull's Eye, I just stayed there to earn all the needed points from that one target and slowly win the game.

I could have thrown at my favorite, higher scoring triples to win it quicker, but my unhurried, methodical, rarely-a-miss drilling at the Bull's Eye was having the desired effect on Larry and Chuck.

The Bull's Eye on a soft-tip dartboard has a louder "clack" sound when a dart hits it in comparison to the other targets. It's quickly followed by a unique, electronic ditty. Defeat in the world of competition can sound like many things but, in a game of Cricket, hearing that "clack" and those subsequent tones is often the game's death knell. They heard this combination of sounds again and again as I refused to throw at anything else, slowly closing in on the win.

Humorously, during the final rounds of this game, a book title from a high school literature class popped into my head. It was Ray Bradbury's, "Something Wicked This Way Comes." The high-drama of the title – relative to this situation – made me laugh to myself.

By the time the game ended, they were both mentally defeated, deflated, embarrassed, frustrated, and downright angry with themselves … and me.

[**Note:** My approach in this particular game runs contrary to the advice I give elsewhere in this book regarding Cricket strategy (see the chapter, "Winning Strategies"). I do not recommend playing competitive darts in this manner … ever. However, in my defense, remember I was being asked to audition here, and as insulting as that was I felt I had earned the right to give a little of it back. Next, this was not tournament or league play. If I had lost this game, it would have meant little with regards to the bigger picture of "making the team." Had I failed to win, I would have merely reverted to the Cricket strategy I normally subscribe to: points first; close later.]

Around eleven o'clock, Larry and Chuck decided I had enjoyed their company far too much for one night, and called a halt to the bloodshed.

It's the mean-spirited part in me that emerged at that point, admittedly, but before they turned to leave I couldn't resist cocking an eyebrow and casually inviting them to shoot with Dale and *me* that coming season. As I stood there grinning ear to ear, they dropped their heads a bit. Only then did they realize it was the "audition" that had motivated me so fiercely that evening. Before Larry answered, sheepish, knowing smiles appeared on the faces of my new teammates. Point made and taken, apparently.

"Yep, that sounds good," Larry replied.

For more information on the power of imagery, resolving issues with confidence, or how to enter "the zone," go to Dr. Patrick Cohn's excellent website which discusses all of these issues in greater depth. Experts in sports psychology consider him a leader in the field of mental skills training for improving athletic performance. Dr. Cohn's Peak Sports website can be found at http://www.PeakSports.com.

Looking Beyond the PPDs and MPRs ...
How to Build a Great Darts Team

"Individual commitment to a group effort – that's what makes a team work, a company work, a society work, a civilization work."
~ **Vince Lombardi**

It is likely there will come a day when you are asked – or drafted – to captain a team of darts players.

While captaining a team involves a variety of secretarial duties (collecting league fees, setting up the dartboard, organizing "team drinks" from the bar, etc.), someday you'll need to draft a replacement shooter or two. Generally, this is a group decision, but most often the captain is the point man who holds the most sway when considering new personnel for the team.

The following are six items to consider when you're looking to build or draft replacements for your team.

Have a Common Goal
You don't need teammates who have all of the same goals. You need teammates who have at least one *common* goal. What is the goal for your team? It's easy to say, "Our goal is to win first place," but not many teams can realistically make this their objective.

Perhaps the goal could be smaller and more individually oriented. For instance, the team could agree the goal is to improve each individual's PPD by a half point, or their MPR by .25. Set goals the team as a unit can adopt, and then agree on the consequences of failing to meet that goal. Make the penalty fun and slightly uncomfortable for the losers, but remember to keep the goal at the forefront of every match.

Many teams have a common goal of shooting together at big, upcoming tournaments. League play can be a great place to lay the groundwork for this. Finding a common rhythm and being able to compensate for each other's weaknesses is part of the learning process that pays big dividends for pre-existing teams who attend these bigger events.

In my darts community, there are three big events which players like to prepare for throughout the year: the Illinois State Darts Tournament (in Springfield or Peoria), Team Dart in Las Vegas, and Bullshooter in Chicago. If there are big tournaments on the horizon where you live and you've got a group of players in mind you'd like to shoot with, ideally, getting them all on one league team to shoot as a unit for a season beforehand is the underpinning to a great showing from everyone.

One Team, Similar Commitments

Good teams are built with members who have the same level of commitment. A player who requires you to regularly find a substitute is not one that is committed enough for the group's benefit. Teams that have an individual or two with lackluster interest, or other interests, tend to pull apart easily.

In my experience, this is a common killer among many teams populated with great players. One member who is disinterested or has obligations that will take him away from playing regularly is distracting enough for the overall success of the group. Two players like this are enough to put the season in jeopardy.

Make sure your mates are responsible individuals with a clear schedule for the upcoming season or tournament. Few things are more distracting for a captain and his or her mates then finding and fitting in a substitute player – even temporarily – who has little experience with the rhythms of shooting with the other members of the team.

Find Teammates Who Can Afford to Play

Let's admit it: Playing darts isn't cheap. While it might not be as expensive as golf, darts players still need a minimum of $20 a match to cover league fees, buy their games, and enjoy a beverage or two.

Some players in my leagues drive an hour one-way so they can qualify to play in the bigger tournaments (a minimum number of games must be played in an affiliated league to be eligible for these). Depending on fuel prices and the vehicle, the gasoline alone can cost them $10 a night.

Consider players who you know can support their darting pastime. Many things, aside from sudden unemployment, can affect this. Divorce, a new baby, a new house, or a car that needs to be replaced are just a few factors that will affect a player's ability to meet his obligations with the team. A good captain will reflect on these things when scouting prospective players.

Gather Players of Similar Averages

Think long-term when building a darts team. Ideally, you'll want to find players with similar abilities who can grow and improve together. The goal of the team should be to cultivate players who will shoot well together for a long period of time, not just one season.

By gathering players who have similar averages, you don't run the risk of having a really poor player dramatically weakening the team's ranking, while you avoid a really good player who leads the team to victory regularly but is looking to jump ship when the season is over. In either case, ultimately, you will face the nearly always unpleasant task of replacing players sooner rather than later.

In the mid-1990s I had a team where all the players were constants for five seasons. That team was probably the best

I've ever been a part of, not just because we got along, had common goals, were committed, and could afford a night out, but because we were rock solid and knew each other's strengths and weaknesses. During one of those seasons, week after week, not one of our four players was less then twelfth on the stats sheet out of some thirty players. We weren't the best in the league, and we were certainly not the worst, but one of our greatest weapons was our consistency. Better teams who played erratically against us usually lost.

Build a Team with Individuals You Like
Since my early days in darts I have made it a mission to gather good *people* around me first, and good *players* second.

Everyone loves to win. I'd be a liar if I said it was unimportant to me. However, my outlook on this is – while I am rabid about this sport and love victories as much as the next guy – first and foremost, darts is a social thing. I'd rather surround myself with good people and lose, then dread league night week after week because there's a brash idiot on the team who – it just so happens – can hit the T20 at will.

Communication and Problem Resolution
If there is an incident that has the potential to disrupt the future of the team (i.e., a drunken episode, a fight, etc.), I've found it is best to have an informal discussion on a "practice night" to reinforce the group's goals and direction. Wives, husbands, fiancés (whoever!), should stay home and let the team hammer it out alone. While it's best to get everything out in the open, too much input from others outside the group is not conducive to resolving problems or insuring the group's future.

Remember to be as fair and democratic as possible in your role as captain. In these delicate situations, you should mediate through the discussion's rougher waters, ask key questions for the group to consider, talk less on the whole, and listen to everyone's opinion equally. And remember to keep a level head, despite your personal opinions.

It's also important to remember the most eloquent person among you is not *always* in the right. Simply put, if it smells and tastes like bullshit, it ain't chocolate. Knowing the difference is in the group's best interest, too.

When a resolution appears unworkable, despite the best of efforts, there may come a time when hard decisions must be made to cut an offending member. While it's typical you will agree on the course of action together, you – as captain – will most likely be the hatchet man. After the group has made its decision, it's your job to remain firm regarding the majority decision. Remember, you are taking action not just for yourself here, but also for your teammates who expect and deserve good, firm leadership.

Bottom line: Individuals with similar goals, similar levels of commitment, similar averages, who can afford to play, whose company everyone enjoys, and who can work together to resolve problems are what make great teams. Pursue like-minded people to fill your roster and, remember, if players don't enjoy their time together, it's not a team ... or, at least, not one that will last long.

Clothes That Can Break Your Game

"Mama says they was magic shoes. They could take me anywhere."
~ **Forrest Gump**

The Shirt

Believe it or not, your shirt is an important consideration when it comes to your better efforts in this game.

The "Bowling" Shirt

To begin this discussion, let's take a look at the traditional "bowling shirts" we've seen on some players in darts leagues and tournaments. Conceptually, the designs of these shirts are perfectly suited for darts because they allow loose and unencumbered movement for your arm as you throw. However, aside from the fact there are better fashion statements out there, show-up at a crowded tournament with one of these 80/20 polyester beauties and you'd probably only sweat more water-weight if you were wrapped in cellophane. Remember, getting over-heated can tire you quickly. My advice: if you like this style, hunt for 100% (or predominantly) cotton material as your best bet.

Next, plain and simple, certain pullover shirts are cut improperly for our sport, can drag your arm down (be it ever so slightly), and tire important arm and shoulder muscles more quickly. This gradual fatigue can cause your throw to change minutely over the course of a long match or tournament. A player that does not recognize the need to adjust to the subtle, physical changes that occur due to these factors will usually find their game unexplainably in the dumpster by the end of the night (alcohol not included!). If you intend to wear a simple cotton t-shirt, know that no two brands are cut the same.

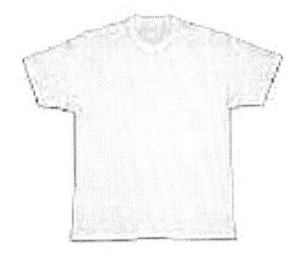

The "Boat Anchor" Shirt

To demonstrate my point, take a look at the first t-shirt picture at left. Notice its design bows down to the sleeves from the collar. This is what I call the "boat anchor" shirt. With rounded shoulders and shortened armpits, this shirt will put too much drag on the arm as we throw ... unless it's way oversized. For darts players – as we hold our throwing arm up, elbow forward – this type of shirt can lead to fatigue during long matches and tournaments, especially if we tuck the shirt into our jeans. When it comes to consistent throwing, this design can certainly work against us in the long run.

The Proper "T" Shirt

This next shirt is the one I normally wear and recommend: a true "T"-shaped shirt. Take a look at the line from the end of the sleeve, through the shirt's collar, and out to the other sleeve's end. Notice it's much straighter? This shirt will not pull at your arm (or your waistband), providing comfort for many hours of play.

Finally, I don't consider myself a fashion guru, so understand it is not my intention to suggest throwing well means you have to "dress down" and wear a t-shirt. Here, we've simply established that the best shirt designs for darts players are truly "T" in shape.

"It's Got To Be The Shoes!"
First and foremost, your shoes must be comfortable enough for you to wear for long periods of time, otherwise you may discover you are tiring much faster then your opponents.

Considerations: Your toes need room to breathe, as they are integral to maintaining a steady balance. Specifically, there should be plenty of room in the end of your shoe for your toes to extend properly. Placing your weight on your forward foot (a common stance) causes that foot to spread. It is natural for the foot to attempt to displace your weight in this way. As most players lean toward the board, the weight of their entire body is directed down to mere inches on this forward foot. Without a proper shoe you are limiting the ability of your foot to spread properly and, more specifically, inhibiting the function of your toes in helping you stay balanced and steady through the forward movement of each throw.

Next, you must have shoes with good arches. Any regular tournament player will tell you that the focus and concentration during matches, then the long waiting periods in between, can be mentally and physically draining enough. Add to these the problems from a pair of shoes with little or no arch support and, well, you can watch your noble attempts at Bull's Eyes "drop into the three" late in the day. Avoid this fatigue by purchasing shoes with good, proper arches. You would hate it if a regular opponent of yours discovered that you were consistently less of a threat after the first few hours of play, even if he doesn't know why!

Personally, I have found that cross-trainers, with good arch supports and a flared sole, work best. Nike used to produce a shoe called the Waffle Trainer back in the late 1970s when I ran track in high school. The interesting aspect of this shoe was that the outer sole was flared wider and longer by about a half-inch beyond the dimensions of the inner sole. They also provided good quality arches since they were built to take the pounding of running on most any type of surface, whether it was a cinder track, hard packed trail, or pavement.

Unfortunately, over the years shoe companies have discovered that few consumers outside the running community actually research purchases involving their feet. Therefore, manufacturers know consumer buying decisions are based not on how the shoe will hold up in the long term, but on three things: 1) price; 2) how the shoes look, and; 3) how the shoes feel the first time they're tried on. How they will feel on your feet next week is irrelevant.

Bottom line: Wear shirts that don't pull your arm down. By laying them out flat you can see the difference between the "boat anchor" shirt and the one shaped more like a "T." Also, for those of you who care to do a little research, there are plenty of excellent, fashionable, long-lasting shoes available like Nike's Metal Max. I don't mean to give Nike any undo publicity here, but these shoes are tough, lightweight, support your feet properly, and can weather plenty of abuse in the arch. While this shoe may be out of production by the time you read this, it is likely they have created different models that are similarly tough. But, do your homework through Consumer Reports magazine, surfing Google, or Epinions.com first! No two shoe models – even from the same manufacturer (yet priced similarly) – are guaranteed to be the same quality.

Know Thy Opponent

"The race is not always to the swift, nor the battle to the strong."
~ **Ecclesiastes 9:11, Bible**

To understand your competition in the easiest way, pour over the stat sheets provided by your league coordinator. Study the names and numbers found there. Where do you fall in the mix?

Next, set realistic goals to overtake those ahead of you, and make it your business to remember player's names and faces in the leagues and tournaments you participate in. If you are new to the league and tournament play in your area, always introduce yourself to your competition and begin taking mental notes about them. Ask what town they're from, do they know "so-and-so" … whatever it takes to help you remember them and build a rapport (after all, these are competitive *and* social events).

Knowing your opponent means not just knowing their averages and the level of skill they bring to a match, though. There is much more to a player then mere numbers can provide. You must take some mental notes regarding everything you can about them. Are they weak on a particular target? Do they lack an understanding of strategy or the Freeze Rule? Can they count their way out of an '01 game in two and three darts? Everyone has weaknesses, but finding these is sometimes difficult. Some are simply more apparent then others.

The Angry Player

Perhaps the shooters you will encounter (and may have already) have personality traits that, at first, don't appear to be weaknesses. For instance, I know some players who cannot shoot well unless they are gnashing their teeth about something/anything. Part of their routine is to get whipped into a very bad mood before a match begins. This is what helps them stay focused and driven. In my opinion, this motivation is cheap, makes the evening difficult to enjoy for everyone, and deserves any tactic I can use to break it. And, yes, anger is also a weakness.

With regards to this type of opponent, if I know their favorite music, I will play it on the jukebox. If I know their favorite drink, I will buy it for them. If they have a hobby, I will feign interest. If I know they have children, I will ask about them ("out of the ballpark" effective). If they've lost weight – and even if they haven't – I will tell them they look great. The point is to nullify anger as a motivating factor in players like this. Distract them from it! Anger is a powerful – yet ignoble – mental trick these shooters have learned to use effectively. When you encounter someone like this make it your mission to step up, not letting it go unchecked.

I will admit I have been able to defuse the angriest players quite effectively when the need strikes me. If this makes me a cutthroat, do-whatever-it-takes-to-win player, at least I'm the nicest cutthroat player you'll ever meet.

The following are other examples I've encountered where exploiting weaknesses or seizing opportunities during match play have occurred. Some of these illustrations are humorous, some are rather mean, some are subtle, and some not so subtle.

The point is that these are all cases of people interacting with each other and having fun, while playing much more then a mere game involving tiny arrows and targets. Indeed, any sport is much more then just its scoreboard. Learn the importance of that last sentence. After all, at the end of the contest there are winners and losers. Staying within the realm of good sportsmanship, if you can learn enough about your opponent and their weaknesses, the winner might as well be you!

"Captain! One Minute to Self-Destruct!"

In the late 1990s, I shot against an opponent/friend I'll refer to as "Dave." He was a pretty good player. In fact, Dave's team was filled with players who were probably – talent wise – better then mine. But my team always beat them. Always.

Whenever he played against me, I noticed Dave tried way too hard to play well. He would over analyze himself, and attempted to control each of his throws far too much. He wanted to beat me (and my cocky attitude) so badly he could taste it. The harder he tried to keep mistakes from happening, though, the more they occurred. Knowingly, I would contribute to this crippling, self-analysis as he came back from the board by commenting on one of his blown opportunities.

I knew Dave was likely already berating himself for it, but I'd jokingly say something like, "You keep working on that triple-four, Dave. It'll come around for you soon enough."

Invariably, he'd smile, shake his head, and look at his darts as though there was something wrong with them, but inside I knew he was cursing himself for shucking one so far out and looking badly. As the night progressed, knowing I was assessing each off-shot he made was only adding more ingredients to the "bad soup" he already had cooking on the stove.

Fortunately enough for my team, when he played against us, Dave always "died on the vine," as they say. The harder he tried, the worse it got ... with some help from me, of course. And, since he was the best player on his team, the rest of his mates ultimately rode the "down wave" with him, too.

I worked Dave over during that period because he *was* good. There were nights – as I watched him shoot against other teams – where he could make a Bull's Eye or a triple absolutely cry in pain. Add to this, based on their individual stats, I knew the combination of players on his team had every potential for being a real threat to the hard-fought ranking my team enjoyed in our league whenever we met up. Dave was simply the key to short-circuiting that threat.

Brother, Beware

Do you have an acquaintance that loves to compete against you? I certainly do. A good friend of mine, Rod Grant, and I really enjoy a healthy, competitive rivalry. We tend to bring out the absolute best in each other, whether it's working out, free throws (at which I suck), table tennis (at which I don't suck), pool, or darts. To say we've thrown some miracle darts against each other … well, you'd just have to have been a witness to believe them. Trust me, the board would smoke when we were finished.

One league night, in particular, he was asked to substitute for an absent player on a team my mates and I were scheduled to shoot against (my team's name was "Second Place Sucks," by the way). His sudden appearance easily made him *the* shooter on their team, and he made it very clear he intended to kick my butt repeatedly with his feats and wins until I begged for mercy.

Not lacking my own bravado, I "roostered" back at him that, when he woke up next week after the severe darts beating I planned to serve up, he should give me a call. To listen to us tell the tale of what was about to transpire – smiling the whole time – you'd have thought Frazier was about to play against Ali. Fortunately for Second Place Sucks, this great showdown never happened.

Early on, I'd realized this was a big night for us, as we were only in first place by a very slim margin. The third place team – for whom Rod was a substitute that night – was positioned as "spoiler" to our first place rank if they could win the match and if the second place team was able to inflict their own, predictable damage elsewhere.

Since Rod was on the home team, his captain was required to pick their player rotation first (thankfully). Once complete, I reviewed it, and then slotted the lineup for my team.

Knowing Rod was capable of throwing very well, especially against me, I purposefully placed myself in a position where we shot against each other the *least* number of times that night. All of the big talk I had been dishing out was merely for show, a complete bluff.

To accomplish this, I was able to use the league's odd way it alternated players in the course of a match to our advantage, and selected my placement so that Rod and I played each other in only three of the seven possible games (of a thirteen game match). Fortunately, not everyone was aware of the score sheet's line-up imbalance, but a big "darts geek" like myself enjoys trivia like this, so I was lucky enough to know how to line it up and, admittedly, chose the "low road" to avoid the challenge.

Battling Rod tooth and nail for seven games would have been a threat, not just for the match win that night, but for my team's first place ranking, too. It may even have been enough by the end of the season – as tight as the first two teams were to each other – to put us in second place. Therefore, with his sudden presence as an opponent, the possibility of losing this match became a serious concern.

As our two teams braced for the big showdown, no one even noticed what I'd done in the lineup, not even my own teammates. My intention, when he appeared in the mix of opposing players, was to sneak past Rod's team and come out on the other side of the match with an even *bigger* stretch of wins then what I'd anticipated before his appearance. Here's how:

Rod's desire to crush me was the key. Remember, I knew him very well. He was a dangerous player and, truth be told, could be supernaturally accurate when properly motivated (i.e., he was *always* motivated against me). Therefore, while I was shooting well enough to make a respectable showing against an onslaught I knew awaited me, I purposely slipped his noose and avoided the battle.

Trust me, though, the few games where we played against each other felt like hell itself had come to visit. Few times in my darts career have I felt the need to bless myself mid-game but, looking back, it happened more then once that night, I'm certain. While our two '01 games were relatively quick and painless (I always appreciate a quick "death" in these situations), our Cricket game was so long and the battle for point lead so thick, I wouldn't have doubted anyone had they told me there were scorch marks on my body afterward.

However (and this is what I was banking on), in those games where I was absent, Rod's level of play was noticeably lackluster. You could tell he was not nearly as interested in them. Since he was not a permanent member of his team, he had no long-term interests in their success, either. His sole motivation was to beat me in every game we played each other. Too bad I was seldom at the line against him. Thinking back on it, he reminded me of a favored-to-win thoroughbred left to trot around the track alone after the other horse no-showed.

Thank goodness we were not the home team that night, with Rod's captain left in control of slotting players against each other as *he* saw fit, or the season could have ended very differently for us (yes, ultimately, Second Place Sucks took first place).

Being able to place myself away from Rod as much as possible, my team was able to rally a huge win, 10-3 … losing only the three games he and I shot against each other. In the face of a very possible 7-6 loss, my shooting against him as few times as possible proved to be the path to victory – not only for that night – but for the season.

What Are Friends For?

Some time ago, I had a teammate we'll call, "Bill." He was a good darts player and, in particular, was absolutely on fire one season. He became our shooter, the "horse" who carried the team to victory repeatedly despite the consistent, humdrum showing from the rest of us.

On the last night of the league, we needed to win seven games to capture first place and win the league. Since our opponents currently held that position, we needed every win we could muster.

Before the match, we were all warming up (we'd probably consumed two beers apiece by then) when one of the players from the opposing team, "Joe," called Bill over to the bar and engaged him in light conversation.

"Here, let me buy you a shot," Joe said, and ordered up a drink for each of them. "We'll do a 'traditional' toast later," he announced, laying the groundwork for what was to come.

Clinking their glasses together, they both downed their drinks. Of course, Bill felt obligated to reciprocate the favor, and bought them each another shot.

Afterward, they exchanged back slaps and pleasantries as long-time friends often do, and Bill went back to the board to warm up for another fifteen minutes before the match.

Now, note that Bill had had two beers and two shots at that point in a very short period of time. No big deal, right? The night was long and the early boost of drinks would help calm the nerves. Right?

But there was something brewing here that Bill was not aware of. You see, the younger (and, even he would admit, sometimes naïve) Bill weighed approximately 165 lbs. Joe, on the other hand, weighed closer to 225 and was better prepared, physically, to tolerate that much alcohol. Add to this, while Bill was definitely the "shooter" on our team, Joe was definitely *not* the shooter on his. The two of them drinking in this way had a greater adverse effect on us then it would on them.

Meanwhile, as we approached game time, remember there was this other, "traditional" toast coming, too.

Back at the bar, Joe asked the bartender to give him a set of house darts (all the same color, please, so as not to raise any suspicions) and ordered two shots of Ouzo. When Joe's team captain announced the match was about to start, Joe stepped up to quickly toast the "traditional" with Bill.

Bill accepted the drink, and asked, "Okay, how do we do this?'"

After his brief "here's to good times, good friends, and good darts" toast, holding all three darts in his hand in a way so Bill couldn't tell they were merely house darts, Joe dipped these fakes into his own drink, removed them, and tossed back the Ouzo. Bill did the same with his real darts, unknowingly.

If you've never had Ouzo, it is a strong, clear, very sugary, black-licorice tasting beverage (quite ugly, in my opinion, but popular enough, nonetheless). And now, right before the match was to commence, Bill had dunked his darts into it, covering most of each barrel with this very, very sticky liquid.

Wiping them off, the match commenced. But after throwing with them in the first round, the tackiness left behind on the barrels caused Bill to miss the board with all but one dart. Rinsing them off seemed to improve things a little, but Ouzo is pretty resilient in its gumminess. Touch any place that still had some residue left with your fingers and you've reintroduced the problem again to your barrels and your throw. Add to all of this, Bill – our shooter, our horse – was showing more and more effects from all the alcohol as each minute ticked by.

And so it went. I'm not even sure we won three games that night, to tell you the truth. It was such a bad beating we didn't even keep our second place ranking, but fell to third, instead.

Looking back on it, it was all quite hilarious. I just wish it hadn't happened to us!

The Customer Is King

A friend of mine used to be the manager of a pool and darts bar in my hometown, where his raises depended on increasing bar business. We'll call him, "Bob." To help accomplish this, he wanted to encourage some great darts shooters to frequent his bar regularly on the assumption other shooters would follow them there, and increase his business, overall.

Throwing darts caught Bob's interest, too. After much practice, he became quite a good shot. He came along so quickly, in fact, he was soon leading his team in the stats and placing rather highly in the league, overall.

On the night of this story, Bob's team came up against the first place team, rife with some excellent, veteran players. As it happened, I was practicing on a board close by and was able to watch the following events transpire:

The match was scheduled for twelve 301 games with a 501 finisher, and Bob opened up the night very hot. His first game was an eight-dart out, while his second game was a perfect, six-dart out.

Soon, after Bob's third win, the veteran team realized he was on a roll and they had to do something quick to take the wind out of his sails. But what could they do?

Distracting him while he stood at the line was too flagrant a foul, while goading, challenging, and antagonizing him away from the line drove him to shoot even better. The veterans were looking at losing for the first time that season, unless they could stop Bob immediately. How could they break his concentration?

Then they hit upon a plan. The key to it was the value Bob placed in keeping shooters of their caliber happy. Before that night, Bob had made no secret about his intentions for the future of darts in his establishment, and the veterans knew his raises were dependent on keeping the likes of them happy.

When Bob returned as player one in his fourth game, he opened with another hat trick. After pulling his darts from the board and turning to happily knuckle his teammates, he noticed that the opposing team – every player – was gone. One went to the bathroom, one went to the bar, one went to make a call on the pay phone, and the last one went to the supply counter to buy some tips.

They stayed away for ten minutes. What affect do you think this action had – not on "Bob the Darts Player" – but on "Bob the Manager?" With not one member from the veteran team saying, "We'll be right back" before they'd left, Bob began to worry. I heard him ask his teammates if the other team was mad about something.

"We don't know," came the general response. "They all just got up and left."

Now, the wheels began to turn in Bob's head. To no one in particular, he asked, "Have I offended them somehow?" He laughed slightly at the thought, albeit insecurely. "What did I do?" he wondered.

And when they didn't return immediately, he fretted even more. He needed the help of these veteran players to make his bar the "shooter's bar" he'd dreamed about. He also struggled with the thought that perhaps he had, somehow, offended the very people in this sport whose respect he wanted.

The more he talked about it with his mates, the more anxious he became. By the time the tight-lipped veterans returned, he was beside himself with worry ... and that was all it took to break Bob's focus.

Although he opened that game with a hat trick before the disappearance, Bob and his mates lost that one and every game afterward that night. He simply could not regain his composure. The veterans, by merely walking away mid-match, had allowed Bob to self-destruct in his own pool of doubt, and orchestrated a "come from behind" win, 8-5.

Remember, it was perfectly legal for the opposing team to take the short break, as there are typically no time limitations in league play. And while this strategy may have the opposite effect on other players, it worked against the Bull's Eye thumping, yet customer-conscious bar manager.

He had been "worked" by seasoned players who knew which buttons would send Bob over the edge. By focusing on this small chink in Bob's armor, they were able to change the course of the match. Here, their tactics away from the board proved very effective.

The Greatest

Of course, when it comes to knowing your opponent, one of my all time favorite examples comes, not from the world of darts, but from boxing.

I make a few references to boxing and Muhammad Ali throughout this book. He has been a hero of mine since I was a boy. And although he oozed self-confidence and was a major boxing talent (with an equally huge mouth), he was a thinker, too. Good Lord, when it came to understanding his opponents, he was a *dangerous* thinker.

In October of 1974, perhaps Ali's greatest career achievement came when he reclaimed the heavyweight title in Zaire, Africa (this twelve year old writer sat riveted, watching as it was replayed on ABC's Wide World of Sports in January, 1975). It is a battle that is over-played, overly talked about, and analyzed by sports junkies in bars, on TV, and in the print media to this day. It remains one of the greatest, most inspiring underdog stories in the entirety of sport.

Ali, to state it simply, should never have won "The Rumble in The Jungle." Against the boxing world's current heavyweight title holder – the still-rising, looming, juggernaut known as George Foreman – Ali should have withered on the vine, suffered a career ending defeat, perhaps even died a horrible ringside death like Jimmy Doyle at the hands of Sugar Ray Robinson in 1947. The odds against him were enormous. Like Norton and Frazier before him, Ali should have crumbled under George Foreman's hammer entirely.

Remember, this was not the gentle George television audiences know today, the smiling grilling magnate, the minister, the jovial corporate spokesman. This was merciless George. This was enraged George. This was "I'm coming to your house and I'm bringing Death with me" George. He was truly formidable. In recent boxing history, only the ferocity of Mike Tyson's "pre-Buster Douglas" career can compare.

For some time before the fight, Foreman and Ali shared a gym in the palatial digs of Zaire's President Mobutu. Although they had different schedules, witnesses claim the echoes of Foreman crashing into the heavy bag would reverberate throughout the gym, low and thunderous.

"Th-oom! Th-oom!! Th-oom! Th-oooom!!!" came the sound, like the footfalls of some tyrannosaurus rex hunting the heroes in a Jurassic Park movie.

For weeks before the fight, Ali endeared himself to the people of Zaire by training in the streets and using these forays to taunt his future opponent repeatedly in the press, as only he could do. Foreman, humorless as he was in those days, seethed at every word.

Pound for pound, no one in the world – past or present – could crush ribs like Foreman in the 1970s. His fists were akin to wrecking balls hitting the side of a dam in a mad hunt for water. In the opening rounds, at any moment you expected just one punch would finish Ali off, leaving him to slump to his heels, then collapse to the mat, eyes open and blank, mouth agape. This is what the odds-makers had predicted would happen. This is what everyone believed would transpire. How could it not? Foreman had dispatched Norton and Frazier handily where Ali had struggled tremendously against those two fighters.

People were truly afraid for Ali when the first round's bell sounded, and watched in horror as those truck collision-like blows began to – as expected – rain into his body. Those at ringside would swear they could hear Ali's breath evacuate his lungs loudly at each landing. The huge, coma-potential, roundhouse swings at his skull barely missed their target, with only Ali's quickness and skill keeping him ahead of these.

Remember, there was no one stronger then George Foreman in boxing, no one bigger. He was so indomitable, no fight had lasted longer then two rounds in the previous three years. Of his 40 professional fights prior to Ali, Foreman won them all – all but three – by KO or TKO, and those three he won by unanimous decision.

But if Ali couldn't out-muscle Foreman, perhaps there was another way? Defending himself and laying on the ropes round after round to conserve energy, Ali would pepper in punches that "angered the beehive," only to hold on and tie-up Foreman's hulking frame to tire him further. Foreman's face had begun to swell from Ali's abuse. And as Ali held on to the big man, he would also ask questions like, "Is that all you got, George?"

The strategy drove Foreman mad with frustration. By the fifth round, it was apparent Ali was directing the flow of this bout, not Foreman.

For all his talent and strength, it was Foreman's pride and rage that was his weakness. Ali was simply smart enough to see this and used it against him. *Ali knew his opponent.* To combat strength and fury, patience and frustration became his weapons. But could Ali absorb such brutal punishment and outlast the big man? This was the question.

As the rounds progressed, Ali's flourishes began to coincide with each of Foreman's more and more sporadic shows of strength, as if Ali knew when to bait the big man again and let him wear himself out with more of those powerful (if exhaustive and inaccurate by then) blows to Ali's body. And Foreman - infuriated by this very vocal, smaller, former champion who refused to fall - took the bait each time.

In the end, the tornado, the hurricane known as George Foreman, simply blew himself out and was reduced to losing his title at the feet of boxing's master thinker. Furious George, for the first time in his professional boxing career, stared upward at an opponent from the mat.

To see this great story told, you should watch the Academy Award winning documentary, "When We Were Kings." On the topic of knowing your opponent, it is truly inspirational. I highly recommend it.

"Ali! Boma ye!" indeed (see the film for the translation).

Bottom line: As we've shown, darts is not the only place where using an advantage or chipping away at weaknesses occurs. It happens in every arena of sport.

Note that not everyone you play against is compromised after a few drinks, or the manager of a bar, or chronically angry, or one of your best friends and competitors. You simply have to discover your edge and use it to your advantage. Be observant and be patient, but most of all remember to be a good sportsman.

Winning Strategies

"He is neither a strategist, nor is he schooled in the operational arts, nor is he a tactician, nor is he a general. Other than that he's a great military man."
~ **General H. Norman Schwarzkopf**

While I can provide advice on basic strategy, this does not take into account any of your opponent's strengths or weaknesses. The ability to blend strategy and your knowledge of what your opponent brings to the line is critical if you are to win in darts.

Let me give you an example: You know your opponent well and are aware – in Cricket – he is weak on 16s and 18s, but hell on 19s and 17s. How does this affect your approach to beating him? If you haven't thought about it before, you should! In this example, my order of closure ("closing a number" means: to register three marks on a target) against this opponent would be: 20-19-17-18-16-15-Bull.

Therefore, take the following information at face value, knowing you may have to bend the rules to address a unique asset or shortcoming a particular opponent brings to the game.

Cricket Mantra: Points First, Points Win

The best, most basic nugget of advice I can give regarding strategy in Cricket is this: Develop and maintain your point lead *first* before closing any other targets. It's that simple.

In tournament or league play, if you are behind on points, simply closing numbers is fruitless work. It is imperative that you point to get ahead first, and close open numbers later.

When it's all said and done, after all marks have been closed, the guy with the most points will win the game every single time. In the event of a tied score, the first to close all 21 marks is the victor (this is a very rare result).

In my many years of playing darts, I have watched in horror as members of my own teams have failed to shoot correctly, tried to be cocky, or be "the hero" by closing numbers first and pointing later. This lacks good judgment and shouldn't ever occur with veteran players.

Unfortunately, it does.

Rallying the Opposition

Usually, if any of my teammates were guilty of this crime, they knew better but just couldn't control themselves (I've been guilty of this, too … see the chapter, "A Tale From Inside 'The Zone'"). To close first and point later is foolish work and can even show a lack of regard for your competition. I've certainly watched this type of cavalier attitude rally the opposition to a win more then once. Avoid this type of "slight" toward your competitors like the plague. Invariably, it will come back to bite you.

In team Cricket, it is imperative that you pay attention to the game, do your job, and be a smart player. Your teammates expect nothing less. Point *first* (and maintain that lead) and close your numbers *second* – 20 thru Bull's Eye – to finish the game as quickly as possible.

The Pro and the Protégé

Recently, I teamed with a friend of mine for a few knock around games of Cricket against a pro-ranked darts player and his "protégé." The pro was hitting targets at will, so to make the contest more of a challenge for him, he'd leave our point generating number open, close all the others, then return to close the open number before we could "point pound" the score (and the game) beyond his reach. The protégé, not knowing any better, followed suit by closing first and pointing later. With the pro player leading the charge, their quick work around the board, then – in the end – generating the needed points on those we'd left open, was pretty easy fare.

To his credit, the pro had helped to develop the protégé into a player of very good accuracy. However, when I quizzed the younger player on why he played the game in this way (close first, point later), it was obvious he was never taught simple Cricket strategy. Ultimately, when paired against a similar or stronger MPR talent in a tournament, by playing incorrectly, the protégé should lose the majority of these matches against anyone who knows the basics.

Scoring and the Point Lead

Now, if you understand the needs of the first round, you can carry it through the rest of the game, like this: If you are the first shooter in the game, closing and scoring sixty points on the 20 target is the ideal minimum effort. Why? In this way, you not only have a point advantage, but have also caused your opponent to spend all three of his darts on the 19 if he is to take the point lead. If he only throws a six-mark on 19s, you still have a point lead. If he throws a seven-mark or better on that number to take the point lead, he still hasn't had the opportunity to shoot at 20s and stop you from pointing and closing appropriately in the next round.

As a good rule of thumb against mid-talented, non-professionals, you should try to stay over three-marks worth of points ahead of what your opponent could possibly generate with one dart. For example, if it's possible for your opponent to generate 54 points with one dart, you'll want to stay at least 55 points ahead before pulling your darts from the board. When possible, always try to make him spend at least two darts to out-point you.

Against pro-level or high-talent players (assuming you are still the new player this book is directed toward), a 100 point lead is a minimum goal. After achieving this point difference, split your objective between pointing and closing open targets in the same round. For instance, let's say you are 103 points ahead. Take the opportunity to shoot one dart for more points and two to close numbers. If your opponent begins to close the gap too rapidly, shoot two at points and one to close. Use your best judgment to maintain and protect your point lead.

Remember, everybody has an off game. Pro-level players are human, too, although some of them would like to make you think otherwise. The best players in the world make mistakes or have bad days, so it's up to you to take advantage when you catch them.

Do not be outright abusive with points, though. There is no need to rub salt in an open wound unnecessarily when the same thing could happen to you in the next game.

Whether you agree with the "point first" strategy or not, *pretend* as though you do and play accordingly! If you elect to close first and point later, simply put, veteran players will clean the bar with you.

The Exception

One of the very few instances where I would hazard to close a number before generating a point-lead would be if I were ahead on marks and just barely behind on points. Here's the scenario:

You have closed all numbers up to, but not including the 16. Your opponent has jumped ahead to this number and is making a valiant stand on it, nailing its triple regularly and staying just ahead of you on points. Meanwhile, he has two marks or less on each of the 20, 19, 18, and 17 targets. You realize it will take a single dart from you to gain the point advantage again, but you elect to spend your remaining darts on closing the 16 instead.

Why was this the right thing to do? Because, while he maintains a point lead, he will need four darts the next round (having only three, of course) to close those open numbers. Meanwhile, you'll be able to make up the points on his still-remaining open number(s) in the next round, and shift the point momentum – and the game – in your direction again.

This is why Cricket is such a chess match. It's a parry and thrust type of game, where every round brings new gambles and opportunities. Don't be a high-stakes player though. While those big risks that produce wins (rare) can be deeply satisfying, keep your speculative efforts "close to the vest" and play conservatively. You'll win more often this way.

The Bull's Eye and Cricket

I recently read a darts book where the author tells of throwing at the Bull's Eye on occasion before the end of the game in an attempt to keep his opponent confused about his strategy. Without pointing out this author (I enjoyed and agree with 99% of his book), I disagree with this thinking, and here's why:

First, strategy in Cricket is not that difficult to master. Shooting at the Bull mid-game against a player who understands strategy, with a variety of targets still at your disposal, will either insult and motivate him (as though you have a lack of regard for his abilities), or simply make you look foolish.

Second, the Bull's Eye should be left for the end of the game for a few reasons. There is no triple on this target, and its double is simply too tough to hit consistently by even the best of shooters. Let me use an example to illustrate:

Pretend a shooter is so accurate on the double Bull's Eye he can hit it at will. Pretend his opponent is equally accurate on T18. It would take two darts to close the double Bull's Eye and score 25 points there, whereas it would take two darts to close the 18 and score 29 *more* points then his Bull's Eye-shooting opponent. Add to this, the T18 is a much larger target then the double

Bull and you can begin to see the senselessness of choosing to throw at this central target when there are bigger, triple targets around the board to mine for greater rewards.

If a player shoots at the Bull's Eye mid-game against you, either he has a huge ego and is attempting to fluster you, or doesn't know much better. Don't let it rattle you, even when it's most likely intended to.

The Freeze Rule

When new players first hear about the Freeze Rule in '01, most can understand it when explained, but can't remember the details while at the line. At best, they only know to ask someone when they get within striking distance of a potential win. That's where I hope this discourse will help. It's really not as daunting as it might first appear.

The Freeze Rule was designed as a handicapping mechanism to keep the partner-oriented, four concurrent scores, '01 game a *team* game, meaning: even though everyone shoots on their own score, you cannot win without the contributions of your partner in the overall effort.

To help you understand the Freeze Rule better, let's break it down into three, individual points:

1) Do not take into account your own score with regard to the Freeze Rule (a popularly confused point).
2) If your partner's score is **more** then your two opponent's combined scores, you are frozen and winning the game is not allowed.
3) If your partner's score is **equal to or less than** your opponent's combined scores, you may win the game.

Actually, to make it even less complicated for you, if you can only remember the third point you'll have an excellent grasp of this oft-confusing element of '01 team play.

That being said, I feel obligated to warn you to be careful in your leagues and tournaments. If you are frozen but accidentally throw a dart to "win," some boards will simply return you to the score you held at the beginning of that round, letting the game continue until a player legitimately reaches zero points. These boards are – arguably (just watch it happen and learn what the word "arguably" means in your community) – not setup properly. Know that, if you are in a sanctioned National Dart Association league, having the score merely returned to the value you had at the beginning of the round is contrary to their rules of play. A player who is frozen, and who takes out a game, should lose that game. Period. Before you get drawn into a confrontation, it's best to know if the boards you shoot on are in accordance with NDA guidelines regarding the Freeze Rule.

Knowledge is Power ...

... but knowledge *shared* is just not appreciated by many players. Few things are more insulting to an experienced darts player then to offer them your advice on strategy where none was sought. My advice is to keep your advice to yourself, unless asked.

If you don't agree with how your partner handles a particular situation, take a moment later when you are both away from the "heat of battle" to discuss it. Whether you feel a decision he made cost your team a game is really a moot point after it's happened. Pointing it out to him during match play will likely be so distracting to his focus in the coming games – even if he's right and *you're* wrong – the hole in the bottom of the boat you are attempting to plug will leave you both treading water in no time.

Now, let me qualify this point: Having captained many teams, I've had players who are both not as talented as the other members, and who have little concept of basic strategy. For the benefit of the team's success during the season, I accept that it is my job to protect wins when they are at risk by these players and make the necessary calls accordingly.

The difference between this and what I've told you above with regards to giving advice is this: As captain, I tell the whole team at the beginning of the season I'm going to reserve the right to do this (the better players know I'm not talking to them, anyway). In this way I'm not singling anyone out, have reserved the right to make decisions to secure wins for the entire team, and can help lessen some performance robbing anxiety in these weaker players by making the more critical decisions for them.

Let me give you an example: Two of my players were in an '01 game, with the weakest player shooting first. This weaker player had a tendency to drop a dart into a triple instead of hitting a single in clutch situations at the top of the board and, with a single dart left, was looking at a single-20 to win the game (note: this player was also not strong enough to toy with the D10). A bust would have likely frozen their stronger partner in that round and would certainly have put the win in jeopardy. Knowing the opposing team's next player was not within striking distance of the win, and knowing my stronger player was more likely to cap the game during his next turn at the line, I asked the weaker player to "stay" on 20 points, and not throw the final dart.

Having said all this, a good captain will also ask weaker players to make tough decisions for themselves during games at those points throughout the season when wins and losses are less critical to the team's ranking. Thinking too often for these players doesn't strengthen their confidence or thinking ability, makes them too dependent on you, and denies them the opportunity to experience clutch shots in the heat of a game. In their best interest during these moments, hope that your previous guidance has had an impact and let them fly on their own when it's affordable.

If you can allow a game loss where these weaker players can also learn valuable lessons, this must be done. It's good for the future of the team to challenge them both mentally and physically, regardless of whether or not less important games are lost in the process.

When it comes to captaining a team, there's more regarding issues like this in the chapter, "Building a Great Darts Team."

Bottom line: Darts, like many sports, is a game of percentages. Cultivate a decent knowledge of what your opponent is capable of and gauge his possibilities of success when taking your own, potential, game-altering risks. This will take time to develop, but always remember the opposing captain is making similar mental calculations about you and your team, too. To enhance your ability with strategy, learn the Freeze Rule and your game winning out shots in '01, learn to count in order to win a game or "freeze" an opponent from winning the game in '01, and remember to generate points to provide needed insurance to move forward, close, and win in Cricket.

This and That

"Some people drink from the fountain of knowledge, others just gargle."
~ **Robert Newton Anthony**

Considering there are few things I love more then darts (yes, you may include my wife in this group), I often find myself thinking of parallels in off-topic books that can be applied to our sport. The following are snippets of information I've gathered from a variety of these, including some "on-topic" sources, too. I hope you find them interesting and beneficial.

Robots We Are Not

Without any warm-up at all, when you step to the line, how do you know the precise effort it takes to hit, say, a T20 with your very first dart of the day?

Well, according to F.A. Hellebrandt in his collection of essays on sport skill, "Readings in Motor Learning," it's only the motion that gets recorded in your memory, *not each detail regarding the throw*. Most professional darts players have a knack for retaining this motion information much clearer than the average player. This allows them to replay the memory more accurately and drill that T20 more often with their first dart. The rest of us must resolve ourselves to "feeling out" the target with a dart or two first. Further, Hellebrandt argues that if the brain were capable of recording each minute, muscular detail involved with effort, release, and direction we could all be deadly accurate, leaving the spectrum of skill among players in every sport extremely narrow.

Components of "The Zone"

A specialist in applied sports psychology, Dr. Patrick Cohn states there are five necessary elements when playing in "the zone:" 1) self-confidence; 2) concentration; 3) the ability to shrug off feelings of guilt regarding missed opportunities; 4) developing strong skill patterns through practice, and; 5) self control. While no one *lives* in "the zone," understanding and employing these elements in your game can help you get there more frequently and easily. By the way, again, I highly recommend Dr. Cohn's website at www.PeakSports.com.

The Sense of Touch

Our fingernails, believe it or not, contribute to our sensory information when we hold a dart. Made up of keratin (a hard protein also found in the beaks of birds, tortoise shells, and fish scales), nails shield the ends of the fingers and toes from trauma and serve to protect and augment their delicate sense of touch.

For darters, it's best to maintain a consistent length with your fingernails. A wavering nail length, allowed to grow too long before they are dramatically cut back, will naturally affect our sense of touch.

Touching something with your fingertip, you actually feel resistance between the object you are touching and the underside of your nail. Notice the color underneath your nail will also change from pink to white as you add pressure. This physiological information is processed by the parietal lobe in our brains and helps us to gauge how much pressure is appropriate for any given task.

A nail that is very short allows the tip of your finger to roll upward slightly. This is fine. A longer nail will flatten the fingertip along the underside of the nail and provide a larger area of resistance. This is fine, too. Whether you like to keep your nails short or long makes little difference, as long as there is consistency.

If the length of our nails is allowed to grow too much before they are cut short, this doesn't help us foster a consistent "imprint" where an appropriate level of fingertip pressure (control) while grasping our darts is concerned.

"Balling The Jack," by Frank Baldwin

BALLING THE JACK (bawl'-ing the jack), slang, *v.*: going for broke; betting it all; to risk everything on one attempt or effort

If you love to read well-written fiction and love to play darts, this is the book for you. Even if you've played in only one season you'll be able to draw comparisons from each of the individuals in this book to people you already know. The story and character development found here are superb. I read this 270-page hardback in three days (a rare feat with my hectic schedule). I couldn't seem to put it down.

There are also some rumors this book will be made into a movie with Ben Affleck who – being one of the newer wave celebrity gamblers – is hungry to play the lead.

The following endorsement is from Douglas Rushkoff, author of "The Ecstasy Club:" "If you can't lay down a twenty to win on this solidly told New York story then go back to the two-dollar tables or, better, a twelve-step meeting. Here's the first writer I've encountered in a long time whose prose can drink me under the table." Enjoy!

Throwing Darts on Your "Down Time"

Did you know your imagination could help make dramatic improvements in your game? According to Brian Abernethy, a member of the Australian Coaching Council, by imagining each step of a game (stance, throws, needed outs, etc.), then imagining you've won, you can dramatically improve your level of skill. Studies by Abernethy suggest that through the use of imagery, the neural transmitters, their pathways, and receptors are all ignited as though a player is actually engaged in competition!

Flame Your Nylons
Regarding nylon flights, when you notice the edges are getting frayed and fuzzy, instead of trimming them with scissors, simply run a lit match along the edges (quickly!) to burn off the ends, reseal the flight, and prolong their life.

Key to Success
John Lowe, long-time darts pro and first to hit a nine dart out on national television in England said, in an interview for "Bull's-Eye News," that extensive amounts of tournament play – more so then isolated number drills, friendly competition, or even league play – is by far the best way to improve your game.

By the way, there is some valuable information soft-tip players can harvest, from the "Bull's Eye News" magazine. Check them out at www.BullsEyeNews.com.

Don't Just Know What to Do ... Visualize It!
Drs. Michael Mone and Donald Baker contend that setting *specific* goals for a teammate can significantly elevate the capacity of that player to improve his game, as published in their white paper titled, "Human Performance."

For example, telling a player that he needs two T17s and a Bull's Eye to win the game is much better then a vague "do your best," or "you know what to do." Regardless of how obvious the goal might be, being specific about what is needed can positively influence performance. Helping that player to visualize the goal is the key.

If the player is already aware of the goal, it reinforces what they know to be true and helps them visualize what they need to win. Of course, if they are not aware, it provides enlightenment *and* visualization.

Communication is the key here, but be diplomatic and tactful. Some players, if they are not aware you are attempting to help them visualize, may be offended if they feel *you* think they can't figure it out on their own.

To avoid offending someone (like a blind draw partner in a tournament who might not be familiar with this exercise), perhaps you could feign confusion and simply ask the question: "How can you win this?"

Giving your partner a reason to verbalize the combination out loud is enough to accomplish your goal, leaving their pride intact.

Lengthening the Life of Your Barrels

Barrels have a tendency to lose their crisp definition after time. The more we use our darts, the knurling and general character will tend to become smoother and less distinct. There are a few reasons for this, but only one major culprit.

Yes, oil from our hands contains a certain amount of acidity, and our hands (and feet) tend to sweat naturally when we're pumped up by competition. Acids and metals do not good bedfellows make, and handling our darts for hundreds of hours a year *will* have an adverse, if small, effect. But it's not the major perpetrator here.

Likewise, throwing tight patterns – as the barrels might scrape past each other to embed themselves in the board – is not a big contributor, either.

The greatest, fastest way to erode your barrels is to pull them all from the board at the same time, with one hand. Let's say you shot all three darts at the T18 with reasonable success. Your darts are now embedded in the board in a rather tight grouping. Pulling them out as a singular group with one hand causes the barrels to scrape and grind together. Over a relatively short period of time your barrels will show a lot of wear.

To preserve your barrels for as long as possible, get in the habit early of removing your darts from the board one at a time. Your darts – and your wallet – will thank you.

Lengthening the Life of Your Nylon Shafts
The late, great Leighton Rees (World Cup Singles Champion: 1977; World Professional Champion: 1978; Grand Masters Champion: 1979) suggested in his book, "Leighton Rees On Darts," a nylon shaft that loosely grips a flight can be corrected. Slip a small, 2Ba, o-ring washer over the shaft to close the slots, dip that end into a pot of boiling water for a few long moments, and then move it immediately to ice water. This sudden temperature shock from one extreme to the other, with the o-ring acting as a directional brace, tightens up the shaft nicely, strengthening it, and prolongs its life.

Creating Your Own Talent Surge
Sports performance author Price Pritchett in his book, "you2," makes some keen observations on sports performance. In it, he states that "quantum leaps" in performance cannot be achieved by incremental steps or by practicing "more of the same." A person must seriously shift gears, take risks, and get ruthless when it comes to improving their skill set. These individuals must live and breathe their sport like never before. They must immerse themselves in it.

For us to create this leap in the sport of darts it's important to investigate new strategies, enter as many tournaments as possible, read about the game wherever we can, talk to all the pro-level players you know about your ideas and be receptive to new ones they might provide, pour over every stat sheet you see, and attack weaknesses – your opponent's and your own – from different angles to get past them.

Throwing Darts in Springfield, Illinois

"The church is near, but the way is icy. The tavern is far, but I will walk carefully."
~ **Ukrainian Proverb**

Location: Springfield, Illinois is the state's capitol, located at the crossroads of I-55 and I-72. Situated 200 miles southwest of Chicago, Springfield lies 100 miles northeast of St. Louis, and 195 miles due west of Indianapolis, Indiana.

Population: 113,000

A Few Points of Interest: President Abraham Lincoln lived and worked here as a legislator and lawyer before his tour in the White House, and is buried in Springfield's Oak Ridge Cemetary; The Abraham Lincoln Presidential Library and Museum is a 200,000 square foot complex situated in downtown Springfield, where it was formally dedicated on April 19, 2005 (www.alplm.org); the Illinois State Fairgrounds in Springfield boasts the fastest mile dirt track in the nation (www.agr.state.il.us/isf); 20% of the entire U.S. population is within 400 miles of Springfield; the third largest carillon in the world is located in Springfield's Washington Park (www.carillon-rees.org); in 2004, Springfield tied for 2nd Place as the "Most Polite City" in the U.S. (I like to think darters played an integral part in this designation); Lincoln Memorial Gardens is the site of a beautiful treasure trove of native plants and well-groomed trails encompassing 100 acres of land on the shores of Lake Springfield. The garden also boasts being inducted into the National Register of Historic Places in 1992 (www.lmgnc.com/index.html), and finally; Springfield's Illinois State Museum possesses one of the world's largest Ice Age mastodon collections (www.museum.state.il.us).

So, You're Coming to Springfield, Eh?

Annie and I get the opportunity to travel around the country occasionally, but we are usually frustrated with the lack of information we can find ahead of time on the better darts bars in our destination cities. Too often we end up spending half of our time interrogating the help at our hotel, every cashier in town where we might shop, cab drivers, etc., with the usual laundry list of questions:

1) Is there a "darts bar" in town?
2) Is it steel-tip or soft-tip?
3) How many boards do they have?
4) Do they serve food?
5) Where is it located?

Therefore, in light of the struggles we've encountered just to enjoy one of our favorite pastimes as we travel, and since Springfield hosts well over a million visitors every year, I thought it would be rather negligent on my part if I didn't include some information on the locations that make up our local darts scene. What follows is a partial list of taverns where you can find soft-tip boards (I am not aware of any steel-tip boards still hanging in the city).

I would suggest you take this book with you on your trip to Springfield and show the listing below to the staff at the front desk of your hotel to find out what's closest to you. Or, if you know the address of your hotel ahead of time, you can logon to www.mapquest.com or maps.yahoo.com to help locate the nearest darts location to it.

Please note, this is a partial listing and – as with any establishment in your own town – all the information presented here is subject to change:

Bars	Address	Phone (Area Code 217)
Alamo, The	115 N 5th St	523-1455
Bootlegger's	1220 Toronto Rd	585-0027
Break Time	2941 W White Oaks	698-0918
Brewhaus	617 E Washington	525-6399
California Sports Bar	3028 Stanford	525-4942
Catch 22	11 W Old State Capitol Plaza	522-5730
Curve Inn	3219 S 6th St	529-5860
Fat Cats	125 Mayden	523-2344
Felber's	2203 S 15th St	528-1572
Four Seasons	1901 Truman Rd	525-8765
Froggy's	131 E Jefferson	523-2406
Huds	1630 N 11th	525-8591
Illinois Tap	715 N Grand Ave E	753-9173
J.W.'s Lounge	2266 So 6th St	544-1303
Louie's	3110 Stanton St	529-8922
Mother's	1901 S Grand Ave E	789-7799
Mowie's Cue	1277 Toronto Rd	529-7616
Sammy's Sports Bar	217 S 5th St	789-9803
Shorty's Southside	2203 So 15th St	523-0842
Show Me's	3101 So MacArthur Blvd	546-2800
Spillway Lanes	1025 Outer Park Dr	546-5221
Starship Billiards	2301 Stevenson Dr	585-8888
Sluggo's	2660 W Lawrence Ave	787-6111
Top Cats Chill & Grill	1822 Stevenson Dr	529-4005
Viele's Planet	126 E Jefferson	525-9029

A Dilemma Best Planned For in Advance

Now, while I'm not suggesting darters are routine drunk drivers, I am suggesting we enjoy a beer or two while playing at our favorite establishments. In light of this, if you travel here from out of state, you should know beforehand that Illinois has one of the fiercest DUI laws on the books. Drivers in Illinois are legally intoxicated at .08 BAC (blood alcohol content), and there is some chatter this level could soon be pushed lower to .06. Too, if you pass the Breathalyzer, but fail the field sobriety test, know that you can still earn yourself a DUI.

To put the seriousness of this into perspective, in 2001 Illinois had over 500 alcohol related traffic fatalities, affecting the lives of – quite possibly – tens of thousands of our residents.

That same year there were nearly 50,000 DUI arrests, with Springfield near the top of the list, per capita. There is little question we have an aggressive DUI enforcement program where few are above the law. Not to name names, but a very important, local, elected official's brother earned a DUI citation in 2003! Take my advice: Be smart, be safe, plan ahead, and enjoy your time here.

The current, average cab fare is $1.25 for the first 1/10-mile and 15 cents for each additional 1/10-mile. The following is a phone listing (area code 217) of Springfield's cab services as taken from our local phone book:

AAA Cab - 789-2780
A Diamond Cab - 788-5828
Airport Cab – 741-3029
Checker Radio Cab - 525-1630
D C Cab - 525-1035
Liberty Cab - 525-1982
Lincoln Yellow Cab - 522-7766, 523-4545, or 525-1630
Mid-state Cab - 522-0960 or 522-9039
Mr. Taxi - 522-TAXI (9039)

Note: *The following information contains some suggestions for places to play darts in Springfield, based on my personal experiences. In no way were these entries paid for or otherwise solicited to earn their inclusion here. That being said, the reader should also understand these suggestions are by no means complete.*

Some Locations for the <u>Casual</u> Darts Player ...
On Springfield's south side – **Mowie's Cue** can be found on Toronto Road – just east of the hotels, Cracker Barrel restaurant, and gas station – in the strip mall on the north side of the street. Inside Mowie's you'll find nearly twenty pool tables, air hockey,

a "drugstore" vending machine that dispenses aspirin, etc. (I mention this specifically because I think it's sheer genius to include one of these in a bar), a digital jukebox, various video games, foosball, shuffleboard, and four dartboards. Simply put, there are plenty of ways to entertain yourself. They also have a sales counter to purchase a limited variety of darts supplies. Regarding food, their short menu consists of deli sandwiches which, I'm told, are available until they close at 1:00pm. If you're an all-around gamer, you'd be hard pressed *not* to enjoy your time there.

Starship Billiards on Stevenson Drive has approximately five dartboards and a host of (obviously) billiard tables, too. Drink prices are reasonable and they have a menu from which you can order a variety of food. The atmosphere is clean and professional, and they have a nice showcase of pool cues, darts, and supplies on display near the entrance. Just in case, it might be a good idea to wear a collared shirt and jeans (no holes), as they have been known – in the past – to enforce a dress code.

On the same street, further west in the Laketown shopping mall, there's a great, casual restaurant called **Top Cat's Chill & Grill.** There's literally something for everyone on the menu (my faves are the stuffed Portobello mushrooms). The portions are large and the prices are very reasonable. Plus, they have a pool table, a dartboard, and a small game room for the kids. Oh, and if you're there during the day, say hello to Annie, the bartender. That's my wife!

By the way, and since we're talking a little about food, in 1928 a chef at the Leland Hotel invented a recipe that has put Springfield on the culinary map. The open-faced Horseshoe sandwich began as two hamburgers on two slices of toast, covered with cheddar cheese sauce buried beneath a mound of French fries. Today, you can substitute any number of meats, like breaded (or grilled, or "buffalo") chicken, turkey, or ham. But, the key to a good horseshoe – or "ponyshoe" for the kids – is the cheese sauce. Find the best cheese sauce and you've found the best horseshoe! To name a few great spots to give this tasty dish a try during your stay in Springfield, check out D'Arcy's Pint, Norb Andy's, The Red Coach Inn, and Top Cat's Chill & Grill. Now, back to the local darts scene....

On Springfield's west side – **Break Time** – near Veterans Parkway and Wabash Avenue – is also the host of Springfield's **Funny Bone Comedy Club** (call 217-391-JOKE for information on who's appearing). There are three soft-tip dartboards and a number of billiards tables. They've also been known to have foosball and shuffleboard tables. There is a kitchen on the premises, too, run by Jeffery's Specialty Sandwiches. If you're hungry, you *must* try their Caribbean Chicken Sandwich. It's unbelievably good ... but ask for extra napkins! Break Time is a good, fun environment with loads of entertainment, all in one place.

About 3 miles further north, and on the other side of Veterans Parkway, there is a well-maintained bowling alley called Strike & Spare West with a bar inside called, **Sluggo's**. It's an interesting place with a huge, windowed atrium. I specifically captained a darts team there a few years back because I enjoyed the atmosphere so much. They have access to the bowling alley's kitchen, too, with the menu consisting of pizzas and appetizers.

In Springfield's downtown area – If you are staying at the Renaissance or Hilton hotels there are plenty of nice bars in the area for you to check out. A variety of micro brewed and imported beers are on hand at the **Brewhaus**. It seems there is always good, live music, so you should have no problem enjoying a game or two on their single dartboard.

Catch-22 on 5th St. is downstairs from a bar called **11 West**. With four dartboards, and as many pool tables, this is a great place to unwind at night. They have an excellent jukebox, and the crowds through the week can be pretty entertaining and lively.

Sammy's Sports Bar is another block south and a great place to enjoy a game of darts, a beer, some food, and a ballgame on one of their numerous high-res, flat screen TVs. The atmosphere there is very enjoyable.

A bit further away on Cook St., you may also consider checking out the **State Bar & Grill** inside the Vinegar Hill Mall. The food is great, and hosts a dartboard for you to enjoy before and after your meal.

Some Locations for the <u>Serious</u> Darts Player ...

On Springfield's east side – **Mother's** on South Grand Avenue (previously known as Handley's) sees owner Dan Petrelli continuing the tavern's reputation for being a vital darts hub for the area. For years, the heavy hitters in Springfield and its surrounding communities have frequented this establishment, circulating more darting tales around the bar then there are fish in the lake. There are five dartboards, periodic charity and benefit tournaments, along with the weekly leagues and tournaments. Drink prices are some of the best in the city, and there always seems to be a game on one of the TVs to watch as you wait your turn to throw, with the regular patrons evenly divided between the Chicago and St. Louis sport franchises. In case you need replacements of any sort, they also maintain a modest supply of tips, flights, and shafts on hand for you to purchase, as well.

On Springfield's south side – **The Curve Inn** – near Stevenson Drive and South 6th Street – is open until 3:00am and is located just a block east of the Route 66 Hotel. Owners Ami Merchant, Ray Merchant, and Don Thompson have done a great job in hosting and promoting in-house and traveling darts leagues, along with a variety of charity and benefit tournaments since they took over a few years ago. With a kitchen and short menu available at lunch and dinner, you'll also find seven dartboards, a number of TVs, and one pool table. Outside, they recently added a stage for bands on the weekends with a large beer garden (and another TV). If you show up between 8 and 8:30pm during the week, you can get a feel for the usually high level of darts talent in the room and lay your challenges as you see fit by the time leagues end at around 9:00pm. You'll find a good-sized darts and pool supply case there, too, if you need to purchase any replacements.

While you will likely have a good time at any of the bars listed above, these last two taverns in particular are the current "hot spots" in Springfield. If it's competition you're looking for, I would suggest you call first to see how busy they expect the bar to be that night. If you mention you're from out of town, had the chance to read a little about their establishment in this book, and are looking for some good competition, the bartenders can certainly make the appropriate introductions for you when you arrive. Take advantage of their knowledge. If there is anyone in the building who's known as a "shooter," bartenders (in any town) are a great resource for the inside scoop on the resident talent.

If you'd like more information on the city of Springfield, you'll get a broader idea of our other interesting sights and things to do by visiting: www.Visit-SpringfieldIllinois.com/.

In Thanks

"Sometimes our light goes out but is blown into flame by another. Each of us owes deepest thanks to those who have rekindled it."
~ **Albert Schweitzer**

There was too long a period from the late 1990s to the early years of the new millennium that I was away from the darts community. In a perfect world, I never would have left. Finally, in 2002, I was ready again.

As luck would have it, one day an old friend appeared at my work desk and asked if I was interested in casting off my retirement. I certainly was. Damon Williams influenced more then my return to competition. He has positively affected my outlook on the game of darts again and, ultimately, the completion of this book. It had lain dormant for most of my time away. Many thanks to him for helping me open these doorways once more. He is a good friend.

My wife, Annie, has always been supportive, understanding, and doesn't mind too much when I return from a darts outing in a complete rage when I couldn't make my arm do what my brain feels I am completely capable of. Bottom line, she loves me like no one ever has, without reservation. My heart is hers.

In addition, I must thank my very patient master's partner, Nate "Gabby" Slaughter, whom I feel was thrust into my boat when I returned. Rusty and ill prepared, I barely resembled the stories he'd heard of me, I'm certain. While I have never been a tremendous talent when compared to the crush of state, world, and otherwise pro-level players here, the "old me" makes the "me today" look pale in comparison. His tolerance, support, and friendship are much appreciated during this, at times, grueling return.

Further, I'd like to thank the kinship of players below who have, over the years, helped to create a great darting community in Springfield, IL. They are a special collection of friends I am thankful were still involved with darts – for the most part – when I returned. For those who have passed on or left us for other pursuits, let me take this opportunity to recognize and extend a tip-of-the-hat to them, as well:

Marie Abner	Aaron Hashman	Denise Montgomery
Andy Albright	Bernie Hashman	Terry Montgomery
Bill Alexander	Mike Hashman	Sue Murawski
Lisa Bartulis	Barb Hassebrock	Marty Needham
Dave Bieneman	Brian Hassebrock	Lynn Neal, Jr.
Marcus Binnion	Rick Hesse	Lynn Neal, Sr.
Rich Bonnett	Dave Higgs	Sharon Neal
Denise Bridwell	Eric "Tic Tac" Hirstein	Sean Nelson
Ernie Brust	Mark Horton	Joe Nielsen
Bob Campbell	Angie Howe	Ronnie Norman
Brian Carrier	Jay Huston	Teri Ostermeier
Josh Ceperich	Denny "Bite Me" Hughes	Dan Petrelli
Doug Cockrum	Nate Irwin	Dennis Pilbean
Kim Conaway	Greg Johnson	Rod "The Dome of Doom" Porter
Craig Crawford	Les Johnson	Rodney Prichard
Mitch Cronister	Todd Jones	Jeremy "Dog" Rees
Carrie Daykin	Scott King	Brian Rhodes
Terry "TD" Denler	Larry Kennedy	Clyde Richardson
Vanessa Durbin	Bob Langdon	Vicky Richardson
Chuck Eades	Lynn Langdon	Colleen Rosenthal
Rhonda Edmonds	Cheryl Lercher	Steve Rossman
Rick Edstrom	Karl Lercher	Jim Schroder
Kenny Fitzgerald	Lisa Livingston	Mike "Shag" Shaughnessy
Robb Fletcher	Alan Lorton	"Honey" Lynn Spencer
Kevin Fowler	Patsy Loveless	Greg Stratton
Darren Frantz	Terry Luster	Mike Stuart
Dale Garlits	Steve Mack	Tricia Stuart
Stacey Garlits	Suzanne Maddox	Sam Theivagt
Gerald Ghant	Todd Maddox	Don Thompson
Alex Glaub	John McConnell	John Vanleer
Don Goodall	Vince McCrory	Wynn Walker
Rod Grant	Mary Margaret McGrath	Brian Williams, Jr.
Marty Green	Ami Merchant	Cheryl Williams
Nancy Grosenbach	Ray "Cupcake" Merchant	Chuck "Part-Time" Wyzard
Mark Gumble	Dave Mihelsic	Ruth Anne Wyzard
Chuck Hagerman	Mike Mihelsic	Robb Yeager
George Hartman	Mitch Miller	Dennis Young
Jennifer Hartman	Scott Miller	Brian "Zito" Zimmerman

Of course, there have been countless teams, leagues, and tournaments these last 14 years. To remember all the faces and names, as some of you can probably attest, would be next to impossible. If I have overlooked someone here, please know it was unintentional.

Upon reviewing these names, I realize some special recognition should go to my first darts team, a group of guys known collectively as The Widowmakers: For you, what may have been a simple night out with friends became – for the first time in my adult life – an opportunity to belong to something exceptional. Your easygoing, good-humored, relaxed friendships were a bright spot during a very difficult time, and words cannot quite make clear my gratitude for it all. Simply put, again, thank you.

With regards to the pre-production of this book, I want to thank my brother-in-law, Mark Suszko, who has provided some invaluable input, direction, and caught some outright factual errors before this book went to press. From a "new player's" perspective, his questions and comments pushed me to be clearer on some ideas, terminology, and history I wrongly assumed were universally known. It's certainly been awhile since I was a new player myself, so I sometimes plodded onward while forgetting to make things clearer or provide necessary background on a topic. Mark's gentle "tapping on the snout" regarding these oversights were greatly appreciated. Thanks to him, this is a much stronger piece of work.

Finally, I must shine the "thank you" light on Mark's wife – and my sister – Jane Bucci, who created the cover art for this book. In the past, Jane and I have collaborated on software and video products for a company I'd worked for, and she also designed the masthead for the college newspaper I edited in the very early 1980s.

Therefore, in light of my long-standing habit of lassoing her into my projects, it is with particular fondness her artistic contributions are a part of this endeavor, too, my first book. To those of us who know her ability, she is a huge talent who is – by her own hand – under realized. In a world where artists of her caliber earn big contract dollars, she's chosen the noble road of being a full-time mom, instead. In this regard, taking time away from her family to complete this project with me deserves a special, heartfelt homage from her little brother. This book looks awesome on the shelf because of her. Thanks, Chain.

The Official Player's Guidebook of the National Dart Association

This document is reprinted courtesy of the AMOA National Dart Association.

Preface
The AMOA National Dart Association (NDA) is the sanctioning body of electronic darting dedicated to the standardization, recognition, promotion and growth of competition worldwide. Memberships are processed without regard to race, color, religion, ethnic origin or age.

Foreword
This player pamphlet entitled "Player's Guidebook" has been prepared for the exclusive use of the members of the NDA. Areas of copyright are protected.

Topics covered in this pamphlet are to be viewed in two ways. First, there are areas of standardization that require compliance of NDA-sanctioned leagues.

Secondly, there are areas that have been included herein that are suggested means of conducting local league play. In all of these areas your local NDA Charter Holder will have full and unequivocal authority to implement rules for league play. Examples of those areas are: Protests; Fines; Forfeits, and; Fees.

We hope this pamphlet will be an asset to you in maximizing your enjoyment of the fastest-growing recreational sport in history: "Electronic Darting – The Game You Can Count On."

AMOA NDA Requirements
Dart Machine Specifications/Installation
8 ft. (96") from Face of Target to Front Edge of Foul Line

5 ft. 8 in. (68") from Floor to Center of Bull's Eye

Note: The measurement is from the "Foul Line" to the "Face" of the dartboard and not from "Foul Line" to the front of the machine cabinet.

Dart Equipment Specifications
Tips used must be standard factory issue for Electronic Darting and cannot have broken tips.

Darts may not exceed eight (8) inches in length measured from end of tip to end of flight.

Darts may not exceed NDA standard for Officially Sanctioned NDA Tournaments. The current weight standard is 18 grams (local standards may vary for leagues and tournaments).

Throwing Area
The area directly in front of the assigned dartboard, not to exceed either dartboard to the left or right of the assigned board, is considered the official "throw area." Up until the time a player has thrown a dart, he/she is allowed to leave the throw area. Once a dart has been thrown, a player is not allowed to completely leave the throw area to the rear or the side. Partially stepping on or placing one foot over the back or the side does NOT constitute a foul.

The "players box," located directly behind the foul line, is reserved for the players competing in the match. This area is considered part of the throw area. The only player allowed in the box is the one who is currently shooting. Any player who completely removed himself from the throw area has indicated that his turn is complete.

For wheelchair-bound participants, the torso can be on but not across the foul line.

Proper Throwing Technique
You are allowed to stand at the Foul Line with your foot no farther than the front edge of the line. A suggested stance is to have the throwing side of your body toward the board. If you are right-handed, your right foot should be on the line and your left foot approximately 18 inches behind. Lean forward slightly with the right knee slightly bent. Balance yourself with the toes of the left foot. Your throwing arm should be in front of your body and the upper arm at approximately a 45-degree angle down, while the forearm is perpendicular. Find the center balance of the dart and hold it lightly. This should be comfortable; you do not need to use all four fingers. The throwing motion should be from your elbow out, holding the upper arm as motionless as possible. Bring your forearm back slightly and with one fluid motion throw the dart toward the target. Remember to follow through by pointing your index finger at the area to which you threw.

General Rules of Play
Players stand at the "throw line," 96 inches horizontally from the face of the dartboard. It is legal to lean over the line. They may step on, but not cross, the line.

Players may use their own darts if they meet the following specifications:

- They must be plastic-tip darts.
- Flights may be any length as long as they do not exceed eight (8) inches in total length.
- Flights may be no wider than ¾ inch as measured from shaft to flight edge and may not have more than four wings.
- Complete darts may not exceed 18 grams in weight.
- Darts may not have broken or cut off tips.

- Darts will be inspected upon request.

Each player throws a maximum of three darts per turn. Darts must be thrown only when the machine instructs to "Throw Darts" and the proper player's number is lit.

It is not required for a player to throw all three darts on every turn. A player may pass or throw fewer than three darts. A player will always be allowed to throw all three darts unless a foul occurs.

Any dart thrown counts as a throw, whether or not it is registered on the machine. A throw counts if it misses the board and bounces out, or if it misses the board completely. A player may not throw the darts over. Dropped darts may be thrown again.

Darts on the board may not be touched until the turn is over, the "Player Change" is activated, and the machine recognizes the end of the turn. Exception: When a dart is in the board and machine reads "Stuck Segment," that dart must be removed by opposing team captain before other darts are thrown.

A round is defined as the period of time from the end of a player's turn to the start of his next turn. On games with stacked teams (players on one score), a round is defined as the end of the player's turn to the start of his/her partner's turn.

Rules of Play – '01
The game is '01 Any In-Any Out. The Bull's Eye will count 50 points.

All players start with 301/501 points and attempt to reach zero. If a player scores more than the total required to reach zero, the player "busts" and the score returns to the score that existed at the start of the turn.

When a player reaches zero, the game is over. The winning team is the team with the lowest combined score (both team members). If the game score ends in a tie, the player/team that reaches zero wins. If a player reaches zero when he is "blocked" or "frozen" he will not be credited with any individual feats (4RO, 6DO, etc./5RO, 9DO, etc.) and the win will be credited to the opposing team as a team win only. All general rules of play will apply.

Rules of Play – Cricket
The game of Cricket will be played with a double Bull's Eye.

The object will be to close the numbers 20, 19, 18, 17, 16, 15 and Bull's Eye in any order before your opponent(s). The player/team that closes all numbers and the Bull's Eye first, and has a greater or equal point score, wins.

An outer Bull's Eye will count 25 points, and an inner Bull's Eye will count 50 points. All general rules of play will apply.

Fouls
The following items constitute fouls. Committing a foul may lead to loss of turn, loss of game, loss of match, expulsion from tournament or league, expulsion from site, or expulsion from future leagues or tournaments. The tournament officials identified by official NDA credentials will make all decisions concerning fouls without specific penalties. The penalty for fouling, unless otherwise stated, is loss of turn for the fouling player.

Adherence to all general foul rules is required.

Fouls must be called within the round in which the foul was committed.

Distracting behavior by opponents while a player is throwing is not allowed and constitutes a foul. Throwing on a non-coined machine is considered a distraction.

On a thrown dart, the dart must make contact with the board before the player's foot makes contact with the floor in front of the throw line or a foul has been committed. A player must receive a warning from the opposing captain. If the problem continues, a referee must be called to witness the foul. If the referee determines that there is a foul, the player will lose his next three darts.

It is each player's responsibility to see that the machine is displaying the appropriate player's number prior to throwing the darts. Play is stopped immediately when the infraction is noticed.

If the game starts and ends in the same order, the game stands as played. If the wrong player shoots in a game and the infraction is noticed before that player has started his/her second round, the game will be started over with the offending team being responsible for coining the machine. If the infraction is noticed after the start of the next game, the preceding game will stand.

If the player throws while the machine is displaying an opponent's number, it constitutes a foul.

If the player has thrown fewer than three darts, the machine is advanced to his correct position by use of the "Player Change" button, and the player is allowed to throw their remaining darts. The game then proceeds normally with the opponent shooting next and so on.

If the player throws all three darts on the opponent's number before the infraction is noticed, the player has completed his turn and the machine is returned to the proper order (the opponent's number) and the game proceeds normally.

If a player throws out of turn and ends the game on that turn, his team loses that game.

If a player throws when the machine is displaying the number of that player's partner, it constitutes a foul.

If the player has thrown all three darts, his turn is completed. The machine is then advanced to the correct player position and play resumes, except that both players from the offending team lose their next turn.

If a player has thrown less than three darts when the infraction is noticed, the machine is advanced to their correct player position, and he is allowed to throw the remainder of his three darts. The machine is then advanced to the correct player position and play resumes, except that both players from the offending team lose their next turn.

Manually scored points
Points scored manually on an opponent's score constitutes a foul. Advance player change button to the correct player position and continue play, except that the player who committed the foul loses his next turn.

Points scored manually on a player's own score constitutes a foul. Advance player change button to the correct player position and continue play, except that both players from that team lose their next turn.

If a machine resets due to power failure or other reason beyond control, the game will start over (replayed from the start).

If a player reaches zero in a round in which that player or that player's partner committed a foul, that player/team loses the game.

Any machine reset, tilt or malfunction due to intentional or non-intentional player action shall result in loss of game for the team committing the action.

Abuse of equipment, poor sportsmanship or unethical conduct as judged by a league director or tournament official may constitute a foul.

Any player/team that commits three fouls in one game will forfeit that game.

Any player found to be using overweight darts or otherwise illegal darts shall cause the team to forfeit all games in the match that player has played. The match will then continue with all players using legal darts. Any protest about weight of darts must be made before completion of the 3rd game and will not be allowed once a match has been concluded.

Disregard of any rules may constitute a foul, and all decisions by referees or tournament committee will be final.

Scoring on the Electronic Darts Machine
The score recorded by the machine is the score that the player receives. The players accept that the machine is always right. The only exception will be on the "Last Dart-Winning Dart" that meets the following criteria: The "Last Dart-Winning Dart" must stick.

If the dart does not stick and the machine awards the win, the machine is right and the game is over. If the machine was displaying the "Throw Darts" message and all other rules were followed then, even if the machine fails to score, or scores incorrectly, the player/team will be credited with the win in that game. Example: Player's score is 24 at the beginning of his turn. His first dart hits and sticks in the single 9 but does not register or score. His second dart scores a single 15, leaving the player on 9. The third dart is then thrown in the single 9, but does not register or score. Since it was the "Last Dart-Winning Dart," that player/team wins the game.

A dart that sticks in the board but does not activate the electronic scoring may not be manually scored.

If there is any question as to whether the machine is scoring or working properly, **STOP THE GAME**. Do not remove darts or activate the "Player Change" button. The team captains must try to solve the problem. If they are unable to do so, they will need to call for service. If the situation cannot be resolved, play will need to be moved to an available board. Scores will be re-entered and play will continue. In tournament play, a referee must be called to resolve the problem.

If a dart bounces off the board it is considered a dart thrown even if it does not score. It may not be thrown again.

If a dart is thrown before the "Throw Darts" message lights, the dart will not score and is considered a dart thrown. It may not be thrown again.

Official Skill Rating Procedure

Points Per Dart (PPD) and Marks Per Round (MPR) are the official means of classifying and ranking players.

PPD: Points Per Dart is used for all '01 games (301, 501, etc.). To obtain a PPD, divide the total points by the number of actual darts thrown. Example: Player #1 wins the game with his 12th dart. He has achieved a total of 301 points. His PPD is 25.08 (301/12 = 25.08). The winner of the game will use the total points of the game, all other players will use the actual points scored as reported by the machine.

MPR: Marks Per Round is used for all Cricket games. To calculate MPR, divide the total number of marks scored by the actual number of darts thrown, then multiply by three (3). Example: Player #1 wins the game with her 46th dart. She has achieved a total of 59 marks. Her MPR is 3.85 (59 / 46 x 3 = 3.85). Handicap rounds do not count for the players without darts in that round. When two (2) players are partners on the same number, they record their results individually.

To establish a Skill Rating, a player must compete in a minimum of 24 league games in a league season that meets the following criteria:

301 (501, 701, etc.): Any '01 league game played open in/open out with a 50 point Bull's Eye on a 15.5-inch target.

Cricket: Standard scoring Cricket games with a split (25/50) Bull's Eye on a 15.5 inch target.

Player Achievements - '01 Feats
6 through 12 Dart Outs (Abbreviated 6DO, 7DO, etc.)
A perfect game for 301 is accomplished with 6 darts. A perfect game for 501 is accomplished with 9 darts. A 7 or 10 Dart Out occurs when you win the game while throwing only 7 or 10 darts. The same is true for 8, 11 and 12 Dart Outs.

4th Round Out (Abbreviated 4RO)
Winning the game on either your 10th, 11th or 12th dart.

Low Ton (Abbreviated LT)
A score of 100 to 150 points in one turn (A Hat Trick is not counted as a Low Ton).

High Ton (Abbreviated HT)
A score of 151 to 180 points in one turn.

Ton Over
Same as High Ton

Hat Trick (Abbreviated HAT)
All three darts registering in either the inner or outer portion of the Bull's Eye on one turn.

High Out
The highest out score in any '01 game.

Assist (Abbreviated A)
When a player receives credit for his/her partner winning the game.

Win (Abbreviated W)
What a player receives when he/she throws the winning dart.

5th Round Out (Abbreviated 5RO)
Winning the game on either the 13th, 14th or 15th dart.

Player Achievements – Cricket Feats
8 Dart Out and 9 Dart Out (Abbreviated 8DO and 9DO)
8 Dart Out is a perfect game when there is a Double Bull's Eye. 9 Dart Out is a perfect game if there is not a Double Bull's Eye.

White Horse (Abbreviated WH)
Three darts registering three different Cricket triples in one turn that have not previously been marked or scored upon by your team (while there are 9 marks in a White Horse, it is not scored as a 9 Mark. See 9 Mark).

9 Mark (Abbreviated 9M)
Registering three Cricket triples in one turn. This could be three different triples that have previously been scored upon by your team, two triples that are the same and a different triple or the same three triples.

8 Mark (Abbreviated 8M)
Registering two triples and one double (could be a double Bull's Eye) in one turn.

7 Mark (Abbreviated 7M)
Registering two triples and one single or one triple and two doubles (could be two double Bull's Eyes) in one turn.

6 Mark (Abbreviated 6M)
Registering two triples, one triple and one double (could be a double Bull's Eye) and one single, or three doubles in one turn.

5 Mark (Abbreviated 5M)
Registering one triple and one double (could be a double Bull's Eye), one triple and two singles, or two doubles (could be two double Bull's Eyes) and one single in one turn.

4 Mark (Abbreviated 4M)
Registering one triple and one single, two doubles (could be two double Bull's Eyes), or one double (could be a double Bull's Eye) and two singles in one turn.

Crick Hat (Abbreviated CHT)
All three darts registering in either the inner or outer circle of the Bull's Eye in one turn. A Hat Trick in Cricket will register anywhere from three marks up to six marks, depending on whether they land in the Bull's Eye's inner or outer circle.

Assist, Win
Same as '01.

Specialty Achievements
Perfect Attendance
Player participates/plays on every night of his/her scheduled league play.

Captain
Player who is Captain of their respective team.

League Champion
Player/team who is the champion at the conclusion of the league season.

Very Improved
Given to a player whose performance has improved greatly during the league season.

Top Gun
Player who is the top shooter.

5-Year Member
Player who has been sanctioned for five consecutive years.

10-Year Member
Player who has been sanctioned for 10 consecutive years.

1st-Year Member
Player who is sanctioned for the first time.

Good Sportsmanship
Given to a player who is not the best player, but exhibits a good attitude.

Three In A Bed
All three darts registering in the same triple in one turn.

Top Hat
Player who registers the most Hat Tricks.

Ton 80
Player registers three triple 20s in one turn.

Glossary of Terms
Here are some common terms or phrases that you will be hearing as a sanctioned player for the NDA:

Actual Darts Thrown – Counting the actual darts that are used, not passed, in a match. Only approved means of tracking feats for the NDA's Team Dart Tournament.

Blocked – A player is BLOCKED when his or her partner's score is higher than the combined score of their opponents. The player may still throw to get his or her points lower, but cannot go out without losing the game because of his or her partner's high score. The following will result in a loss: When a player reaches zero but his or her partner's score is not equal to or lower than their opponents combined score. Remember you can go out on a tie.

Classified League – Any league that consists of teams with similar or closely matched team averages.

Closed – When a team has scored 3 Marks on the same number or Bull's Eye in Cricket.

Feats – Various darting accomplishments. (See '01 and Cricket Feats)

Frozen – A player is FROZEN when his or her score is at one point (two points in "Double out") and his or her partner's score is higher than the combined score of their opponent's. The player may not get his score any lower without losing the game (See Blocked).

Games – The individual components of a match.

Geographic League – Any league that consists of teams from the same area or location in a town.

Ladies – Teams consisting of only females.

League – All teams that compete directly against each other in a season.

League Division – Teams in a specified combination or skill level.

League System – All of a Charter Holder's leagues.

MPR – Marks Per Round – The system for averaging the marks a player throws each turn in a game of Cricket. The higher the MPR, the better the player.

Mark – Any throw that registers on a number either to help close the number or score points in Cricket. The Single segment portion of the Cricket number scores one (1) mark. The Double segment scores two (2) marks, while the Triple segment scores three (3) marks. The outer portion of the Bull's Eye scores one (1) mark and the inner section scores two (2) marks.

Match – The total games played on a league night.

Mixed Doubles – Teams made up of an equal number of males and females. In each game a female and male throw together.

Open – Teams made up of any combination of males and/or females.

PPD – Points Per Dart – The system for averaging the points a player throws on each dart in an '01 game. The higher the PPD, the better the player.

Passed Darts – Darts not thrown during a round or game for one reason or another.

Round – A player/team's turn during a game. Each player has the <u>option</u> of throwing zero, one, two or three darts each round.

Spot Darts – A way of handicapping players, teams and leagues. Better players throw fewer darts at the beginning of the game.

Spot Round(s) – The first or opening rounds of a spot-handicapped game.

Turn – A player is entitled to a maximum of three darts per turn. A player may opt to throw zero, one, two or three darts.

Unclosed – When a team has two or fewer marks on a number or Bull's Eye.

NATIONAL DART ASSOCIATION
5613 W. 74th Street
Indianapolis, IN 46278-1753
(317) 387-1299 Office; (800) 808-9884 Toll Free
(317) 387-0999 Fax
http://www.ndadarts.com

About the Author

Timothy R. Bucci was born in Springfield, Illinois in 1963. He graduated from college in 1986 with a degree in journalism from Eastern Illinois University. Upon graduation, he began a career in marketing and information technology, and began playing soft-tip darts in 1991. By 1992, as his enthusiasm for the game grew, the notion of writing a book about soft-tip darting began to take shape. Throughout the 1990s, his articles could be found in a variety of darts publications and newsletters. He currently shoots darts in a two-man master's league, chronicling those exploits for a local amusement company in a regular feature called, "Gabby and Two-Toes Go to War." He has a wife named Annie, no kids, and no pets ... unless you count his cockatiel – Flinch – that's presently flying free around the neighborhood.

Printed in Great Britain
by Amazon.co.uk, Ltd.,
Marston Gate.